YOU HAVE THE ANSWER—

There is never a single correct answer to any problem. There is only the answer you choose and the ways you choose to make it work. Nothing would make this old auntie happier than for all of you to learn how to come up with that answer yourselves, and put me out of business!

— Irma Kurtz

IRMA KURTZ'S
Ultimate
Problem
Solver

IRMA KURTZ

COSMOPOLITAN

IRMA KURTZ'S ULTIMATE PROBLEM SOLVER is an original publication of Cosmopolitan Books. This work has never before appeared in book form.

COSMOPOLITAN BOOKS
AVON BOOKS
A division of
The Hearst Corporation
1350 Avenue of the Americas
New York, New York 10019

Copyright © 1995 by Irma Kurtz
Published by arrangement with the author
Library of Congress Catalog Card Number: 95-94485
ISBN: 0-380-77977-3

First Cosmopolitan Books Printing: December 1995

COSMOPOLITAN TRADEMARK REG. U.S. PAT. OFF. AND IN OTHER COUNTRIES, MARCA REGISTRADA, HECHO EN U.S.A.

Printed in the U.S.A.

RA   10   9   8   7   6   5   4   3   2   1

To Midge, for her courage and friendship

Contents

Preface
1

Problem One
*Where Is Mister Wonderful
and What's Taking Him So Long?*
11

Problem Two
What Is Commitment and How Do I Get It?
39

Problem Three
Sex Is Fun. What's an Orgasm?
55

Problem Four
Can There Be Love Without Trouble?
68

Problem Five
*What Are the Odds of Happiness
with a Married Man?*
98

Problem Six
Is Infidelity Ever Forgivable?
111

Problem Seven
Is There Life After Loneliness?
135

Problem Eight
What Are Friends For?
156

Problem Nine
*Patterns: You Made 'Em and
You Can Break 'Em*
172

Problem Ten
*Life Stinks. Why Can't I Feel Good
About Myself?*
186

Preface

Nosy and bossy. That's what you have to be in my line of work. Endless curiosity and an irrepressible compulsion to communicate what I am thinking are probably the two highest qualifications for this job.

On a good day, I am also possessed of an imagination that makes me feel instantly at home in the skin of another human being—and often on the basis of no more than a few handwritten notes to *Cosmopolitan*'s resident advice columnist, or "agony aunt" as I prefer to be called. An agony aunt is what I am: older than most of the people who consult me and, as any good auntie would be, always ready to put in my two cents.

Heaven knows, I've been around. But I am neither an infallible know-it-all claiming to comprehend every emotional hiccough of mere mortals nor an expert on very much more than I have seen firsthand or done or in some instances dreamed. I have no formal training and participate in no school of thought. And I most definitely am not a psychologist, psychiatrist, or therapist.

1

It would bore me rigid to sit silently hour after hour listening to accusations and complaints. Not being able to give a running, spontaneous opinion on what I was hearing would frustrate me beyond belief. My *opinion* is what I offer the people who write to me. And my opinions are based on reason, not a moral code; on what *is*, and never what *should* be.

Although telling people what *is* may not always be politically correct, telling them what they *should* do is hardly ever ethical. ''You should'' too often means ''I want you to.'' That's why I consciously try to avoid the word ''should'' in both my replies to letters and my everyday conversations.

I am also very, very careful to share my honest opinion only with those I love or when I'm paid for it, which is fairly often. I write for my living, after all.

In my role of agony aunt, I have a vast readership on several continents, and it constantly astonishes me that so many people read my words and pay attention to them. As long as they do, I intend to say exactly what I mean and to say it as well as I can. I do not expect you to do what I say but merely to *hear* me out and then, having heard, to do as you decide you must.

We All Need
an Agony Aunt Now and Then

The trouble with trouble is that a body in the middle of it loses sight of the countless possibilities between ''either'' and ''or,'' ''stay'' and ''go,'' ''yes'' and "no." She is unable to distinguish the shades between black and white. And that's where an agony aunt or caring friend with a more detached viewpoint comes in. We point out the choices a troubled woman cannot see as well as (and I'm afraid this is more likely) the ones she does not *wish* to see.

Why won't she see them? Because mankind in general, and specifically womankind, have a practically limitless capacity for self-delusion. Proof of this is in the statements I hear constantly: "He'll change after we're married," for instance. Or, "Of course he still loves me—he has sex with me, doesn't he?" Or, "He broke my heart. It's over. All I want is for us to stay friends. . . ."

This agony aunt can only reply: "Fat chance!" Hope is a virtue, to be sure, but this kind of wishful thinking is the antithesis of what you need to lead a relatively untroubled life.

If the answers to all our problems were as pleasant and easy as we *wished* them to be, agony aunts would be unnecessary. But the truth of the matter is that the most useful alternatives in the long run are often the *least* pleasant, the most difficult, the most solitary, and the ones we most need a friend or an agony aunt to help us choose.

Of course, we all cannot help one another all the time. We don't always know how. Tales of rape, incest, child abuse, mental illness, drug addiction, alcoholism, entrenched eating disorders, criminality, and disabling physical conditions all come my way, but their treatment lies beyond my scope. Some problems are too deep, dank, and dangerous for me or you or anyone without professional training to tackle, and certain young women who write to "The Agony Column" do need professional assistance or could benefit from it. Nonetheless, of every thousand who ask "Do I need therapy?" to 999 I find it safe to reply: "Certainly not!"

Common sense and intuition will tell you when it is time to go for expert help yourself or encourage a friend or relative to find a therapist. But bear in mind that this type of help is not always the most helpful thing to have. The multitude of experts on every little thing hanging out their shingles these days often encourage emotional laziness. By turning to them prematurely or unnecessarily, we become self-absorbed and weaker. We forget just how expert about ourselves each of us can become *by ourselves*.

Most of us emerge stronger and better off when we use our own resources, along with the sympathy of friends or a few words from an agony aunt, to get through emotional crises. And it's only after we've come through a few storms essentially on our own that we can be of any assistance to a lover or friend or child who is counting on us to see her through a rough patch.

Agony Aunts Aren't Angels

Many of the problems that come my way through *Cosmo*'s "Agony Column" strike a chord because I too have been there. I never married (never saw the point of it). I have had a child (well planned but out of wedlock). And more than once in my life, I've made a mess of things.

I have been with men I did not really love, loved men whom I did not much like, and gone to bed with men I hardly knew. I've sent letters I wished I hadn't. Once (and only once) I was involved with another woman's husband. And many years ago, I had to have an abortion. (I still endorse the call for free and legal terminations.)

But has my life been a perpetual building site for another's benefit? Who am I to say? I do know that it is not necessary for us agony aunts to have led blameless lives. For one thing, it would not be very smart of a troubled woman to seek earthy advice from an angel. For another, no spirited woman can stay out of trouble entirely.

Trouble is part of the price we pay for freedom. But learning how to get out of trouble and how not to get into the same damn trouble again and again and again is one of the rewards of experience— which is why you do not need to be good to become wise. Experience taken to heart in due course becomes wisdom. And wisdom is a gift to be shared.

Heeding the Voices of Experience

These are a few of the lessons experience can teach you:

- If you stay with a violent man, don't be surprised when he hits you.

- Excessive jealousy can actually create the infidelity it dreads.
- No eighteen-year-old is ever as mature as she thinks she is (and to think herself mature at eighteen is immature).
- No matter what that straying husband whispers in your ear, you can bet that he still makes love to his wife at least occasionally.

If a born romantic like me has learned how to learn from experience, then you can too. First, you need to accumulate your own body of experience. Next, add to it all you have ever observed or read or heard about the experiences of others. Then, draw logical, clear-thinking conclusions.

Since old wives were young and telling their first tales, women have learned and taught one another by sifting through and exchanging views on their own and other people's lives. In plain language, they've gossiped.

Yes, gossip has a bad name—and deservedly so when it is malicious. Malicious gossip reinforces prejudice without any increase in understanding. However, creative, *benevolent* gossip—observing, analyzing, and comparing the behavior of human beings—uncovers some basic truths about that behavior and gives us general rules to apply in our private lives.

For instance, while exceptions do exist, if you look around, listen to other mistresses or the wives of wandering husbands, and learn that married men continue *not* to leave their wives a lot more often than they leave them, you can safely conclude that the married man you are involved with probably won't be leaving *his* wife any time soon.

Solving Your Own Problems—with Common Sense

Common sense is a defensive skill, acquired rather than inspired, and generally peace loving. Don't undersell it. Common sense has contributed as much as imagination and ingenuity to our survival on this planet. It is available to all, yet used by very few.

There are certain areas where it seems not to apply, though. Love, for example, rarely makes much sense—common or otherwise. And *any* commitment whatsoever—to a mate, a way of life, a religion—requires a leap of faith.

When even the wisest of us commits herself to love, she surrenders all her rationality and common sense to high-leaping faith: in her beloved, herself, her intuition, her luck—and in her ability to pick herself up and start over if she has made a mistake. Her faith is based not only on what she knows for sure but also on what she *believes* or *chooses* to hold as true—and that is never sure. Indeed, there is no greater risk. The woman who wants to be trouble free studies the risks, watches the ground for pitfalls in her path, and keeps on thinking.

To assist you in this regard, I've included a list of questions at the end of each chapter. They are not for scoring or drawing up psychological profiles. There are no correct or incorrect answers to any of them. Their only purpose is to get you thinking, talking, and preferably writing about the issues raised by the problems that come your way.

Whenever I read a letter or listen to the sorrow of a friend, I am reminded of other readers and friends with similar problems. Yet, each has her own handwriting, her own phrasing, and taste in stationery. Sometimes there's even a trace of perfume on the page. These unique characteristics offer clues to her special nature.

Many of the women who solicit my advice are not in the habit of writing their thoughts down on paper. Yet, one of the chief goods I do my readers is to give them a reason to put their tumultuous, troubled feelings into words. In doing so, they can't help but start to make order out of their chaos. Words written down give you a grasp on them that you cannot have when they're spoken into air.

Finally, let me say, giving advice is a funny line of work. The ultimate job satisfaction for me would be for you to do alone what you hope I will do for you when you write to me. By leading you through the problem-solving process I use while reading letters to "The Agony Column," this book encourages you to think your own way through (or over, under, or around) your troubles.

There is never a single correct answer. There is only the answer you choose and the ways you choose to make your answer work. Nothing would make this old auntie happier than for all of you to learn how to come up with that answer yourselves and put me out of business.

Ten Basic Rules for a (relatively) Trouble-Free Life

1. Always keep the real problem at the front of your mind: Don't treat symptoms instead of root causes.

2. Do the best you can. Never expect anyone else to do better than he can—or will.

3. The only way to change another human being's behavior is to change the way you react to it.

4. Love is acceptance.

5. Love is never a reason to accept what is intolerable.

6. You are responsible for yourself. You are *not* responsible for anyone else over the age of consent.

7. You and you alone are your own judge. Be honest, strong, and merciful.

8. Some problems cannot be solved. They can only be left for time to change or carry away.

9. You damn well *can* help the way you feel.

10. Nothing can ever be what it was again. Anyhow, it wasn't the way you remember it.

• • • • • • • • •

Where Is Mister Wonderful and What's Taking Him So Long?

Dear Irma,

I have a successful career in business, a house of my own, a car, and a circle of good friends. I have devoted the past ten years, since I was in my early twenties, to building up my career and financial security. Although I have been involved with a few men, I have never been prepared to really invest time and effort in these relationships because of my career. Lately I've started longing to settle down and have a family. But there is nobody special in my life, and I am worried. Most of the men I meet are married. I have a very dear companion I've known since we were kids. He's divorced. I can see myself drifting into marriage with him. This is not ideal, but the option of being single and childless suddenly terrifies me.

Have all my years of hard work been worthwhile? My life seems suddenly empty.

"Unfulfilled"

With its connotations of permanence and completion and its cozy overtones of "ever after" and "once and for all," fulfillment is a comforting notion, but more fantasy than practical reality, I'm sorry to say. Nothing is perfectly fulfilling, and a certain amount of unfulfillment is part of every existence, no matter how actively or aggressively it is led. Even women who appear to have it all, don't always have it when they want it or have all of it at the same time.

"Unfulfilled" could have more accurately signed her letter "Unhappy." Happiness is what practically everyone means when they say "fulfillment." But fulfillment and happiness are not the same thing. The most fulfilled people in the end are those who have worked the hardest, often giving more than they've received. They have not necessarily led lives of extraordinary happiness, nor been particularly happy at all.

Even during the worst moments of my life, I would not have signed a letter "Unfulfilled." "Unhappy," yes. When I was alone in Paris after my first serious love affair ended, I was definitely unhappy. But "unfulfilled"? The word reverberates with regret. And regret is useless—worse than useless, actually. It keeps a woman looking back at the path she's already traveled. She's so busy judging herself in retrospect that she continually trips over her own feet.

I always try to warn a woman like "Unfulfilled" away from the inclination to regret. The life she was leading felt right until recently. It *was* right for her at the time, and if she had it to live again, she would lead it precisely the same way. So would you. So would I. Knowing no more than we knew then, every last one of us would make similar choices, have similar successes, and fall short of our goals at roughly the same places. We cannot let the mistakes we made or the roads we did not travel in the past slow us down now.

For instance, I was never given music lessons as a child, and for many years an "unfulfilled pianist" moped around inside me. Then, one day when I was in my early twenties and listening to others play, I realized that to listen and not play might not be altogether fulfilling, but it was a whole lot better than nothing.

The same can be said for failing to hook up with Mister Wonderful. I never found mine, and I'd hardly call myself an "unfulfilled monogamous wife." These days, marrying well is not the only success women can anticipate. We are capable of many wonderful achievements that would astound our grandmas.

Of course, no woman dreams that she will end up on her own. The age-old fairy tale in which a princess is awakened (at last!) by the kiss of a handsome prince has been so soundly drummed into women's minds that most are genuinely surprised to wake up at thirty, forty, or fifty in beds that are still half empty. Once the initial shock wears off, though, some of us gamely accept manlessness in middle age as a final hurdle into relative serenity. For others, it actually comes as a relief.

Sex and the Successful Woman

Poor "Unfulfilled." All she wanted when she wrote to me was instructions on how to get a man, and here I am lecturing her on the meaning of fulfillment. If she were right here in front of me, I probably wouldn't bother her with all the abstract stuff I happen to enjoy so much. However, I wouldn't hand her a list of dating agencies either. Whether they're your own or someone else's, problems must be mulled over and specific answers built on a foundation of what you hold to be true in general.

By all means, let us be practical about what ails us. But always bear in mind that practical answers without imagination are rather like a telephone directory: useful in the short term but not very gripping to read or likely to help you solve future problems.

"Unfulfilled" set her own high standards and achieved them. She has a house, job, income, friends. Now unfamiliar urges are begging for satisfaction. She wants a man. Whether she finds him or not, the next stage of her fulfillment, like the earlier one, is up to her.

Regrettably, I cannot give her a metaphorical pat on the head and assure her that a mature woman who is successful in her career can easily run out, grab a mate, and start making babies. Unless she is befuddled by wishful thinking or distracted by what she thinks *should* be, any woman with the slightest power of observation must notice that the serious pursuit of worldly success *does* affect a woman's marital status. You bet your sweet veil and hope chest it does. In the business world, where single-minded determination is the key to success, Mister Wonderful can end up being the ultimate luxury item.

Far be it for me to discourage a young woman from pursuing a serious career if that is what she has a mind to do. But don't let her imagine Harrison Ford clones are hanging around the executive suite looking to get laid. (And even if they were, office romances can cause malicious gossip, envy, tainted office politics, and a whole mass of other problems.)

As an ambitious woman climbs the professional ladder, she has a natural tendency to look at men on her own rung or above it for possible dates. Only, the higher a woman looks for a man, the fewer men she'll find; and as "Unfulfilled" discovered, the few that are there are likely to be married already. Or dating bimbos. Or both.

In addition, there are very few truly "new" men around. Most men still feel threatened when a woman's job status or salary reaches the same level as their own or tops it. And threatened men make lousy lovers.

As negative as this sounds, none of it means that successful, independent, well-off single women might as well give up hope and take vows of chastity. There are still plenty of ways to attract Mister Wonderful and sign him up for life.

In Search of . . . "True Love"

She writes: *"I am twenty-two. All I want is to get married, have children, be in love and be loved by someone forever. . . ."*

I reply: *"Is that all you want? How about a really big lottery win, while you're at it, or a magic carpet . . . ?"*

Maybe there really is one Mister Wonderful for each Miss Right on earth: one man, one woman, circling the planet searching for each other; one nut, one bolt, looking to connect in a perfect screw. If this were true, their chances of bumping into each other would defy calculation.

Perhaps the bleakness of these odds explains why otherwise rational women turn superstitious when it comes to love and are prepared to listen to any stargazer or hairstylist who claims to know where Mister Wonderful is hiding and how to lure him out.

A friend from India thinks "Unfulfilled" and the rest of us are frantic and deluded in our search for Mister Wonderful. "If a man and a woman are both compatible decent people, why should marriage not come first," she says, "and love come afterwards?" Her marriage was arranged for her by her parents.

"Tell me who knows me as well as they do, Irma, or could so much want the best for me?" my friend comments. Her parents introduced her to a number of young men they considered suitable for her. She found one she liked the looks of and, in due course, decided she could make a life with him. She has been happily married for ten years now, practices law, and has two children. I am delighted for her. But I would not advise "Unfulfilled" to run right home and ask her parents to help her find a mate.

Family ties are looser here in the West. In our fast-paced, technology-driven culture, which allows new fashions and forms of expression to spring up and spread practically overnight, young people are constantly rebelling, redesigning themselves, and leaving older members of the family behind. As a result, parents do not necessarily know their grown daughters well enough to select appropriate Mister Wonderful candidates for them.

Besides, "Unfulfilled" probably subscribes to the Hollywood version of romance anyway. She wants to run into Mister Wonderful coincidentally, recognize him instantly, and go off with him in a blaze of glory the way lovers do in the movies. No arranged marriages for her, thank you very much. And none for the less starry-eyed either. There's no role for arranged marriages in a society like ours that equates freedom with having a multitude of personal choices, bewildering as they may be.

At least "Unfulfilled" acknowledges that love affairs require an investment of "time and effort." Agony aunts and other busybodies like me go on and on about how you have to "work at a relationship," because being fulfilled in a relationship is a challenge. Love is not an end in itself. Love is the easy part and only an overture to the endeavor, compromise, and fulfillment that come later.

She writes: *"He's eighteen and I'm sixteen. How can I make my parents understand that we are in love forever. I will never find any other man for me. . . ."*

I reply: *"Never mind 'forever.' If you can love him for another six months, that might begin to persuade your parents. . . ."*

Frankly, I'd rather receive a hundred letters from women like "Unfulfilled" who are in their early thirties and looking for Mister Wonderful than just one from a sixteen- or seventeen-year-old who imagines she has found him. Because every living thing grows and changes, today's fulfillment is hardly ever enough to meet tomorrow's needs. Thus, any girl who hastily commits herself to what feels like fulfillment at seventeen, eighteen, or nineteen is making a decision that will seriously stunt her growth.

What seems fulfilling now may merely satisfy later (and later still can turn into a major pain in the proverbial). Sometimes love at first sight lasts a lifetime without losing its enchantment. More often the flames of early passion flicker, but the love affair survives because two people, knowing they are happier together than not, decide to make the best of the good thing they have. An awful lot of life depends on making do.

How Wonderful Must Mister Wonderful Be?

She writes: *"Where is a Kevin Costner for me?"*

I reply: *" 'A' Kevin Costner doesn't exist. There*

is only 'the' Kevin Costner. And he's a very busy man.''

Some of my readers' requirements for Mister Wonderful are superficial and really very silly. Smoking, for example. Smokers are "bad," they tell me. Nonsmokers are "good." Now, I don't like cigarette smoke myself, especially first thing in the morning. But when did smoking become a moral issue? To my knowledge, smokers aren't inherently violent, sly, or evil. It astounds me that anybody could seriously consider a weakness for tobacco reason enough not to love another human being, or even to despise him. And it gets worse.

How petty and self-centered have we become? Well, nowhere is it written that the male in any mixed pair must be the taller of the two—except in half the personal ads placed by women searching for Mister Wonderful, that is. Even on the brink of desperation, most women still cannot imagine being taller than their dates. Or as a smallish man I know put it after signing up with a dating service, "You women are all heightist."

She writes: *"I am twenty-three and have a good job. I am attractive and intelligent. But I can't find a partner. Every man I meet is either not good-looking enough, rich enough, or intelligent enough. Am I looking for an ideal that just doesn't exist?"*

I reply: *"Good looks change. Poor men become rich. Rich men lose their money. Intelligence lasts, yes, but we can appreciate it in others only according to how much of it we possess ourselves. What I believe you are actually telling me is that you are twenty-three years old and you have not yet fallen*

*madly in love. When you do, it could be with a poor
man who is quite plain and hasn't got a lot to say
for himself. Yet, somehow he will manage to make
your heart turn cartwheels. God alone knows
why. . . ."*

Nowadays, many women writing to "The Agony
Column" refer to their lovers as "partners." "Partner" sounds more solid and serious than "lover,"
doesn't it? More grown-up and feet-on-the-ground.
But it all boils down to the same thing in the end.
Whether a woman calls the man in her life lover,
partner, husband or merely "my friend," chances
are she still wants the poor sap to do everything she
thinks he *should* and take responsibility for her happiness. That's an unfair burden to place on anyone.

It is utter folly to think a man, child, or any other
human being will fulfill you. "Fulfillment" can be
sought *with* a lover—and sometimes *found* with
him—but it's childish and downright nuts to expect
it *from* him.

Nobody ought to settle for less than she truly
needs from a relationship, not on any score. It is far
better to be single forever than disastrously hitched.
But is his taste in clothes, cars, or furniture really
important? How much do the color of his eyes, his
height, and the amount of hair on his chest really
matter? Would you actually reject an otherwise ideal
man because he had a bumpy marital history or children from a previous union? Trust me, these trivial
criteria for Mister Wonderful can be dropped with
no loss whatsoever to the central qualities that are
always cited when women describe their ideal

men—sensitivity, sense of humor, fidelity, and honesty, to name a few.

Some Serious Considerations

She writes: *"Dear Irma, please help! There's this gorgeous guy hanging around under my balcony. But our families are deadly enemies and will oppose the irrepressible love we feel for each other. I am only fourteen, but mature for my age. . . ."*

I reply: *"Dear Juliet, I'm sure you're over-dramatizing the way teenagers always do. . . ."*

Looking for a mate in her maturity instead of earlier on gives "Unfulfilled" one real advantage. She has no doubt abandoned many of the juvenile "must haves" she once linked to her dream man. Requirements for race, religion, social standing, age, education, and income are a bit more complicated, however. To what degree are they a fixed, integral part of her image of the ideal man? Or anyone's?

She writes: *"I'm twenty-one and I've been dating my boyfriend for seven months now. What bothers me is the way people talk about us and look at us when we're together. He is black and I am white. My mother can't stand it . . . and doesn't want anything to do with me. I fear I will ultimately have to choose between my boyfriend and my parents. I love my boyfriend very much. What should I do?"*

With any romance between people of different races the odds against winning the gamble for happiness increase. To start, it is harder to read signals across chasms of culture or upbringing and easier to misunderstand each other's expectations.

Just talk to any mother who has tried to get her child back from an absconding Islamic husband. Ask her, "When you were in the first flush of love, what did you imagine your marriage was going to be like?" Then ask her to tell you how the facts compared to her romantic fantasy. And while you're at it, ask him what made him think that his western bride would understand and be able to conform to traditions completely different from her own.

Then there is the matter of outside pressure.

She writes: *"I am a black single parent. At first everything was great between me and my white boyfriend, but communication between us is failing. I am starting to think he only moved in with me as a way of rebelling against his rich family. . . ."*

My reply begins: *"I salute your courage. . . ."*

In a mailbag full of daydreams, any letter from a writer who actually faces and analyzes an unflattering possibility earns an agony aunt's respect. I'd like so much to assure her that she is wrong to think her lover is using their interracial love affair to score a political point. But how can I? The chances are he is.

I've received plenty of letters from girls who have chosen a Mister Wonderful their family finds unsuitable precisely to sock Mommy or Daddy in the eye. Why should a man not be capable of equally childish and selfish behavior? (Of course, that selfish and childish guy might actually love her. If love required lovers to be perfect gentlemen or even very bright, not much loving would get off the ground.)

Interracial relationships are not frowned upon by

all. When it comes to disparities in the human condition, I have no trouble with racial differences, and I suspect that ''Unfulfilled's'' parents (who are no doubt more desperate for her to marry than she is) and her sophisticated business friends might have few problems accepting her interracial affair with a man of the right status and age. They might be less charitable, though, if she introduced a nineteen-year-old bisexual out-of-work actor as the man of her dreams.

If an adult professional woman like ''Unfulfilled'' wrote to me and said she was on the brink of committing to an underage, sexually ambiguous, underemployed Romeo I'd also lace into her—but to no avail. An agony aunt need not fear that her practical observations will ever dissuade a woman in love from her grand and tragic destiny. In the end, she and she alone decides if—and why—the Mister Wonderful she's chosen satisfies her essential needs. When she believes herself to be as sure as she can be, then it's to hell with me, or anyone else who claims to know better.

Mind you, if it all goes wrong later, she can hardly blame *him* for being who she was too besotted to notice he was all along. And she can hardly blame *me* or anyone who tried to warn her. If anything's to blame, it's love—or chemistry. Knowing that, she can move on with no regrets, some jolly memories, and hopefully no need to repeat the experience.

Nobody is more vulnerable to humiliation than a woman who makes a romantic choice against the advice of people who mean her well. By the same token, nobody is more despicable than a well-wisher who later says "I told you so."

More Differences

Unfashionable as it is to say these days, great age differences can also block long-range happiness. I've found that younger men who choose significantly older women are almost always bone lazy. Just look at all the aging celebrities who waltz off with boy toys, only to end up having their hearts broken and their pockets picked.

Only a lazy guy would be eager to settle into a ready-made life built around *her* success, *her* family, *her* money, and a comfortable future that has cost him no personal effort beyond flexing his pectorals.

Likewise, a girl who falls for a much older man is rarely looking for grown-up love at all. She wants a proverbial father figure, a sugar daddy whom she will, in all likelihood, one day outgrow or discard.

Yes, yes, I know there are lots of exceptions. But for every Oona O'Neill and Charlie Chaplin there are a heap of unions that could not span the generation gap.

On the plus side (yes, there is one), what seemed a vast age difference in your parents' day appears narrower today. Relationships in which the man is nine or ten years younger than the woman or eighteen or twenty years older can work, depending on the relative youthfulness or maturity of both parties.

She writes: *"I met my beloved at college, but now that we've graduated our differences are becoming apparent. The physical attraction is explosive. We can't bear to be apart. I'm from a working-class background. I'm egalitarian, humanist, and want to right all the world's wrongs. He comes from a wealthy middle-class family. His mother is the biggest snob I know.*

He isn't a snob, but one day he'll need a wife to cook dinner parties and arrange flowers and wear Saint Laurent dresses. I could never be that wife, so I suppose we'll have to split up eventually. . . ."

I reply: *"Your beloved is not a snob, you say. Are you? Do you think because he comes from a rich home he cannot be your equal in sensitivity or understanding? That's an odd kind of egalitarianism. All people in love have to come to terms with something. Does he agree with your humanitarian worldview? If he does not and you are truly committed to your principles, then your union will be in trouble after the sexual fire dies down."*

Whether the difference between a woman and her candidate for Mister Wonderful is in age, race, or social standing she can expect to take some flak from outsiders. Perhaps they feel entitled to give it. Marriage, or any formal union between a man and a woman, is a social contract, after all. But even so, people who say, "You could have done better," are simply snobs, and their opinions hold no more weight than a soap bubble.

On the other hand, if a young woman needs to ask me how to get her family or social circle to accept her lover, she may not be as sure of her own choice as she'd like to think. And if my answer helps her decide to give up her lover, then, in the end, public opinion mattered more to her than he. He just wasn't Mister Wonderful enough—which is fair or at least realistic.

Social and parental ties *do* matter. To some of us they matter a great deal. And sometimes they will outweigh romantic love. Somewhere along the line, each of us has to decide for herself which of the cards she was dealt at birth she wants to hold on to and which are safe to throw away.

Is It a Jungle Out There?

Every friend or lover was once a stranger—which is why I have always been a great believer in talking to strangers. But lately I find myself hesitating to recommend it to lonely women. What stops me is not that life has become more dangerous. Life has *always* been dangerous. It's just that women today, especially American women, seem to have lost confidence in their own instincts and powers of observation. We seem no longer to trust ourselves to get ourselves out of sticky situations, particularly if they involve a predatory man.

In my opinion, we cry for help too often and too soon because we have forgotten how to handle unwelcome attention from a raunchy male. What ever happened to the swift putdown? (''If that were mine, I wouldn't show it to anyone.'') What ever happened to self-preservation? (''I *think* I was raped. I was drunk. Does that count?'') What ever happened to common sense? (''He takes drugs in a big way, but don't tell me to leave him, because I love him.'') Is it really necessary for a woman in possession of all her faculties to run to a court of law, have a nervous collapse, or join a victim's group each time she gets in a jam?

A life worth living includes risks, and each of us must learn to cope with them. Yes, terrible things can happen. They always have. But wonderful things can happen too—if you have the guts to take calculated risks. (Nothing at all happens to a girl who doesn't.)

Although there are lunatics and villains who slip past even the most stringent vetting, unless you are completely out of touch with your own instincts you will recognize a lothario or a weirdo practically on sight. Just be sure to meet blind dates for the first time or the first few times in brightly lit places with a crowd of other people nearby. Then listen to your intuition. It was a woman's best defense long before sexual harassment and date rape became high-fashion squawks.

She writes: *"Aren't there any decent men left? I go out clubbing with my girlfriends, and every guy we meet just wants sex. I hate the whole idea of the one-night stand, but that's all there is out there. . . ."*

Although I can't tell you exactly where to find your Mister Wonderful, if you want a lover who's likely to stay beyond breakfast in bed, then I can tell you where *not* to look. Do not follow the lemmings to watering holes where music and booze and friction add up to nothing more than a one-night stand. Only women younger than "Unfulfilled" and newly divorced women whose social lives stood still during their marriages search for Mister Wonderful there (and they get disillusioned soon enough).

Bars and clubs can be fun occasionally, but if the men you meet in those places only want sex and you want more, why not hunt in new territory? Be imaginative. Expand your horizons. Invest in a good time. Go to concerts, movies, parks, libraries, PTA meetings, new shops, new cities, Canada, Alaska, Mexico. Try renewing old friendships, do volunteer work, go white-water rafting. The world is full of possibilities, and some of them are just around the corner.

Where to Look for Mister Wonderful

She writes: *"Irma, I have so much love to give. I know the man for me is out there somewhere. But where?"*

I reply: *"He will be wherever you find him. . . ."*

Mister Wonderful tends to turn up precisely when a girl is not looking for him. I think that's because women actively seeking love seem desperate, and desperation is not sexy. It is also unflattering to the guy she sets her sights on. It suggests she can't do better than him, and that immediately makes him think he couldn't do worse than her. The instant a man senses that a woman might be desperate, she's in trouble. One whiff and the proud, nervous buck leaps off to a new and safer hunting ground.

By the same token, males tend to be quite attracted to women who are otherwise engaged. Thus, when what you are seeking is a mate (or just a date), it's not a bad idea to seek something else altogether. What should that something be? Something you have always wondered about or wanted to try and can undertake with genuine enthusiasm. Enthusiasm is madly sexy. It puts a spring in your step and a light in your eyes that is immensely attractive.

She writes: *"I have joined everything from sky-diving clubs to bridge clubs. . . . I've tried it all, just like you advised. So, why haven't I met Mister Wonderful . . . ?"*

I reply: *"I never said to try it all, only what you want to try. . . ."*

Your enthusiasm has to be real. What would be the point, say, for "Unfulfilled" to pretend she's dying to shoot pool if the truth is, she's only in a pool hall because she figures it's a good place to meet men? A pool hall is a good place to meet pool players, just as midair is where you meet sky divers. If "Unfulfilled" isn't genuinely interested in pool, any guy who *is* interested in the game will take one look at her and see she's a phoney.

I'm not saying she won't get it on with him. Having spotted a fake, he might take what's offered. But chances are slim that he will take it seriously.

Everything we do creates by-products. Whether "Unfulfilled" chooses an activity that is athletic, musical, intellectual, recreational, artistic, or just plain fun, if she undertakes it with real enthusiasm, it's bound to broaden her outlook, increase her confidence, and introduce her to like-minded people. Even if Mister Wonderful does not appear on the scene, she will have enriched her life significantly. How bad can that be?

Try a Little Help from Your Friends

Ambitious women who are organized and busy at work have been steadily narrowing their spheres of activity and streamlining their address books. I'll bet if I asked her, "Unfulfilled" would say she feels as if she has met every friend she will have in her lifetime.

"I used to think that too," I'd say to her, "but then I learned that we never reach the limit of our friendships, not until we have reached the limit of ourselves." Then I'd encourage her to cultivate as many friendships with women as she can.

I won't pretend friendships between females can't engender monumental problems of their own. (Over the years they've accounted for about 10 percent of my mail and a similar percentage of misery in my own life.) On the whole, though, the company of women is absolutely fabulous.

Contrary to popular opinion, when women get together there is very little small talk. Even women who have never met before dive right into intense, meaningful, uproarious conversations about their own lives and life in general. And when women on the same wavelength go out on the town, they always end up having a good time. Only a nincompoop would call a jolly night out with the girls a "waste" just because she didn't encounter Mister Wonderful.

It used to be commonly held that a woman looking for a man was smart to keep away from other women, especially if the other women were on the loose, too. It was also customary way back then for young women to be introduced to their future mates by their families or friends of the family. How times have changed. These days, an independent woman like ''Unfulfilled'' who has long since left the nest must use her own resources to locate potential Mister Wonderfuls, and those resources include her family or friends.

Some of those friends are probably single women who are also in the market for mates. With two or three of them, ''Unfulfilled'' can boldly go where she might feel out of place on her own: to clubs, restaurants, bars, concerts, or holiday resorts.

What's more, a lot of nice guys find it easier to approach a pair or a group of women than a woman alone. A single woman is an unknown quantity to a man—she could be desperate, dangerous, or waiting for someone else. And what if he's misreading her signals? Men can be timid creatures too, believe it or not. They're afraid of rejection, though they try not to show it.

Or Check Out Some Modern-Day ''Matchmaking''

On-line computer courtship, specialized advertising, dating agencies, and other high-tech methods for meeting potential mates save you time and trouble without limiting your freedom to choose who you actually date or end up with. All that is remotely dangerous about them is the unreal expectations of those who apply to them. We women especially tend to lose our critical facilities and sense of balance the instant we encounter the merest hope of romance.

As a general rule (and there is nothing an agony aunt likes more than a general rule), our actions count not for their aims alone but also for the *manner* in which we undertake them. In other words, if "Unfulfilled" decides to try technodating, she will need to see it in her own mind not as a last resort but as the choice of a grown woman who is too busy for traditional dating games.

Is it safe to trust that "Unfulfilled's" business acumen indicates a cool head? I hope so. If she goes in embarrassed, self-conscious, fearful, or dizzily hopeful, she's bound to come out disappointed. But if she maintains her sense of humor, like a tightrope walker's balancing stick, it will see her through.

Making the whole experiment bold, stylish, and amusing will not detract in the least from her genuine intent to find Mister Wonderful—and might even improve her chances. With luck she could find a guy who has a similarly realistic yet cheerful attitude.

Learn to Flirt

She writes: *"Dear Irma, I am falling in love with my coworker. He doesn't know. We are really good friends, and there are times I think he might feel the same way about me. I'm afraid to spoil our friendship. Do I have to leave my job?"*

I reply: *"Desire makes heat and it shows first in the eyes. Look him in the eye, think heat, feel heat, transmit heat, and if he doesn't get the message, he's probably a dud.''*

A while ago I met a woman from Boston who made her living going around America giving courses in flirtation. I once thought that would be a bit like teaching breathing, but these days practically every mail delivery brings letters from women who are sexually attracted to male friends and afraid that they'll ruin the friendship by making a sexual overture.

What are they planning to do, I wonder, throw the guy to the ground and grab his crotch? While I quite agree that sexual intercourse is not exactly an act of friendship, there are plenty of steps before that. So, for crying out loud, unless the guy is married—or you are—or he is gay or seriously depraved, flirt with him. He either will flirt back or he won't.

As for quitting a job if an awkward pass at a co-worker goes wrong . . . is the girl off her rocker? It will all blow over in less time than it takes to tell. And these days another job can be a whole lot harder to find than another man.

You Can Lead a Fulfilling Life With or Without Mister Wonderful

She writes: *"I am thirty years old. I was the only child of older parents who kept me their 'little girl.' My father died when I was in my teens, and I live with my mother, who is blind. I have never had a sexual relationship. . . . I have no girlfriends . . . if I go anywhere, it is with my mother. . . ."*

Some people find peace in a life of service and obedience, but contented people do not write to an agony aunt. I regularly hear from a small but important group of young and not so young women who feel trapped by their obligations and have never had the chance to pursue even the possibility of fulfillment. ''Is it too late for me?'' they ask.

It is neither early nor late, I tell them. It is time to grab their lives and make a break for it. Of course, I recommend they plan their escapes thoroughly and see to it that their dependents receive all the assistance they can afford or our society offers. Never forgetting that long after I have moved on to other letters, they alone will suffer (or celebrate) the aftermath of their decisions, I gently urge them to find the courage to change their fate.

''Unfulfilled'' is actually lucky by comparison. She has her house, her position, her friends. She is free to seek fulfillment wherever she can and in any way she wants. If I thought it would help, I might remind her of those less fortunate who have few opportunities to find any kind of fulfillment, let alone track down a Mister Wonderful. But nobody's tears have ever evaporated because someone else is shedding more of them and faster. And no woman's problems have been solved by dwelling on the troubles of other people who are worse off than she.

''Unfulfilled'' says the option of being single and childless scares her, but there is an even scarier option—throwing in the towel on Mister Wonderful and having a child anyway. Neither marriage nor a stable union is required to produce offspring. Every day babies are made without benefit of wedlock, and not all of those pregnancies are unplanned. I have a wonderful twenty-two-year-old son who proves that. For me, the maternal drive was not cute or cozy or warm. It was raging, fierce, and so hungry it would have eaten me alive had I not found a way to appease it in time.

Organized, independent, self-financed motherhood has been the greatest adventure of my existence. But I did not undertake it casually, and never in a million years will you hear me advise "Unfulfilled" or anyone else to do as I did.

She writes: *"My last date was over two years ago. I'm scared of being alone and childless for the rest of my miserable life. I plan on finding a man to make me pregnant by my twenty-fourth birthday next year or killing myself. . . ."*

To raise healthy, happy children with help is hard; to raise them on your own is harder still. It worked for me because I worked my tail off to make it work. And it brought me nothing but joy because I made a well-thought-out decision beforehand.

The same cannot be said for hysterics who threaten to commit suicide if they aren't pregnant by age twenty-four. I would never want them or similarly excitable girls to read my words as encouragement to spawn alone and heedlessly.

"Unfulfilled" has time to make up her mind about a lot of things. If she decides to have a baby on her own, and I get wind of it, I'll support her to the limit; but she'll have to come to that decision without any urging from me or anyone.

Likewise, if her biological clock is not set to explode, and she never finds Mister Wonderful, her potential to love and be loved can be fulfilled in countless other ways. She can settle into a comfortable match or develop closer ties to her family and friends or, as so many single, childless women from past generations have done, channel her generosity and energy into making the world a better place for everyone.

Dear "Unfulfilled,"

The search for a soulmate is an investment of self—your very own one-and-only genuine 100 percent self. If you must look back, then do it with pride in all you have accomplished and become. All your achievements have turned you into a prize for any Mister Wonderful. (Would you want a man without the wit to know how good you are?)

Bring to bear on the problem of finding your Mister Wonderful all the qualities that have made you successful in your business life: imagination, high but realistic goals, ambition, and organizational and communication skills.

Open up new markets for personal expansion. Be creative about your extracurricular activities. From all the things you've ever wanted to try or learn or do, choose those that will lead you to groups of people outside your own profession or line of work. Why not plan a holiday that will take you someplace new and off the beaten track? In your position, I'd travel alone (in *my* position I'd travel alone; I *like* to travel alone). But if you can't see your way clear to do that, choose your traveling companions very, very carefully. The point is to shake up your nonworking life and let the pieces fall in brand-new patterns. Get out of your rut. Mister Wonderfuls hardly ever tumble into ruts.

Do not panic. A woman in a panic does not merely drift into the wrong relationships. She *leaps* into them like a headless chicken. Advertise yourself if you have a mind to do it. Maybe some great guy out there has signed up for a dating agency or reads personal ads in an oh-what-the-hell spirit just like yours.

And while I have your attention, what about that dear companion you've known since childhood? Try looking at him as if you'd just been introduced. Among the corny, homegrown wisdom that gets passed from generation to generation and proves to be true nearly every time is the notion that what a person searches for far and wide is occasionally (not *always*) right there under her uppity nose. Sensible women want to fall madly in love and then hope love will turn into abiding friendship. Why should it not be just as smart, even smarter, to arrange things the other way around?

Yours hopefully,
Aunt Irma

Agony Aunt's Work Sheet

1. Do you believe there is just one Mister Wonderful for every woman?

2. Is believing the same as knowing?

3. Do you *believe* there is one man for one woman in this life, or do you *know* it?

4. Do you *believe* there is one man for one woman, or do you *hope* so?

5. Even if you think age difference doesn't matter, list three reasons it *could* matter.

6. What are the attributes of your Mister Wonderful, starting with the *least* important?

7. Name something and someone you found fulfilling ten years ago. Do they fulfill you now?

8. How would you reply to "Unfulfilled's" letter?

PROBLEM TWO

• • • • • • • • •

What Is Commitment
and How Do I Get It?

Dear Irma,

I am twenty-three, and met my boyfriend
three years ago. We got engaged but decided
to wait before getting married. We bought a
house together, though (over a year ago),
and I recently brought up the subject of
commitment. He said he no longer wanted
to marry me. He still loves me, but he
doesn't *ever* want to get married. He says I
shouldn't take it personally, but I feel let
down and cheated. I am not prepared to
stick around without security or commitment. I love him, but I don't think I can
stay, knowing he will never commit himself.
The more I try to think things out, the more
in a muddle I am.

"Confused"

"Commitment" is a relatively new word in the world of emotional agony. It gained popularity in the hard-hearted eighties, as I recall. Until then it had been applied to religion and politics more commonly than to personal and romantic attachments. A man was more likely to be a "committed Democrat" or a "committed Christian" than a committed lover. For that matter, he was more likely to be committed to an institution such as a prison or a psychiatric hospital than to the institution of marriage—and marriage is what "Confused" and thousands like her are talking about, whether they use the word or not.

There are stages of commitment, of course, from "pick you up at eight" to "I love you" to living together. But none count for as much as the commitment that culminates in "I do." Like "partner," "significant other," and "feeling good about myself," the word "commitment" conveys less emotion and seems so much more manageable than such tender, old-fashioned words as "lover," "love affair," or "happy." It offers up the utterly deluded impression that we are in control of our feelings and immune to the wild abandon and mad infatuation responsible for many of our past troubles. In some circles, even the word "love" has been discarded, replaced by "care" (as in "I care for you"). Yet, when all is said and done, good old wedlock is still what most women want.

Love and Marriage . . .

She writes: *"If he loved me, he would commit himself for me."*

I reply: *"He does not commit himself for you or for love, he commits himself to you and to marriage. It's not the same thing. Even in love, commitment is not a duty; it is a personal choice. It can be undertaken for its own sake only, not for anyone or anything else. . . ."*

Love requires no commitment whatsoever. It arrives without design and is under no obligation. Marriage is planned and exclusive, however, and intended to last a lifetime. It is a commitment apart from love, and one that young women, perhaps prodded by the primeval *ticktock* of their biological clocks, appear to be ready for more quickly and at an earlier age than men.

The women who write to me have a hard time grasping this concept. A dialogue between myself and one of them might go something like this.

SHE: Why won't he commit himself?

ME: Why *should* he commit himself?

SHE: Because I'm ready for commitment.

ME: What if *he* isn't ready?

SHE: If he really loved me, he would be.

ME: Are you saying he doesn't love you?

SHE: I know he loves me. So, why won't he commit himself?

ME: Why *should* he?

Judging by my mail, young men do not subscribe to the notion that love and marriage go together like a horse and carriage. They do not see commitment as an expression of love or an extension of "caring" the way young women do. In the boyish mind, timing rather than emotion or a generalized zest for nesting seems to generate commitment. In short, it could be he loves the pants off you. But ready to marry, he ain't. And it's readiness, not love, that settles a man down.

When a man is not ready for marriage, it does not necessarily mean he still wants to play the field (though that can be a part of it). It's more likely that he's not yet ready to be like the image he holds of his father: responsible, worn down, aging, and dull.

Many, many young men see commitment—even to a woman they dearly love and are already living with—as the beginning of the end of good times. They equate marriage with surrendering their carefree youths. And until they view marriage as a happy next step, they simply are not ready for it. Some never will be.

She writes: *"He says he doesn't want to marry me and never will marry anyone. I only want him. Should I expect him to be more sensitive to my needs?"*

I reply: *"Want whatever you must and dream on, but what good will it do to expect him to be other than he is . . . ?"*

Women think marriage is good for men. But a lot of men would rather not do what a woman says is good for them. They find it restricting and too much like being bossed around by their mothers during boyhood.

She writes: *"My boyfriend refuses to have sex with me. He says he is not ready for commitment. He says he doesn't mind my kissing him, but when*

I do, he's not exactly enthusiastic in return. Friends say he's just using me. . . ."

I reply: *"What do your friends say he is using you for? He is not your boyfriend. A boyfriend is a man who when you kiss him, does more than just tolerate it. He seems to reject what you offer. And what you offer essentially is commitment. He doesn't want it. . . . "*

More often than not, a woman believes that once a man is married he will change. A bad-mannered boy will become a polite one. A drunk will turn into a teetotaller. She wants him to go from flirt to someone with eyes for her alone or from playboy to provider.

A young man also believes that the sweet girl he loves will change if he marries her. She'll become a wife, who nags, screams, sulks, and does everything she can to change him from playboy to provider, bad boy to polite one, and so on. He just isn't ready for that.

In addition, some uncommitted men oppose marriage as a matter of principle. They are unwilling to involve themselves in an institution they do not believe in. And when the women in their lives argue, "If you loved me, you would . . ." they might as well be saying, "If you really loved me, you'd change your religion . . ." or "vote Republican . . ." or "support my hometown football team instead of your own." It just doesn't make sense.

Will He *Ever* Be Ready?

She writes: *"We've been together for seven years and we have two beautiful children. But whenever I ask him to commit himself, he stalls or gets angry...."*

I reply: *"Seven years and a couple of kids sure sounds like a commitment to me. If, however, you want him to marry you, that's another issue...."*

Lots of men are scared witless of marriage because they have been married miserably in the past or they have grown up in bad examples of the institution. So have women, of course, but they seem less likely to lose faith in love's healing and restorative powers.

From a young girl's perspective, the "happily ever after" of bedtime stories began at the altar. For boys, the fun stuff—the dragon slaying, damsel saving, and swashbuckling—all came beforehand. Freedom, independence, the chance to sail off to new continents or planets, dreams, adventures—indeed all the joys of his youth seemed to *end* with the wedding march.

To be honest (what else?) I have always thought he had a point. One of the reasons I have not been deeply tempted to have affairs with married men is that I find husbands less dashing and attractive than single men of any age. Perhaps that is also one of the reasons I never wanted to marry even when I was in love: Why make a husband out of a free-spirited lad?

Of course, there is always common-law marriage or other equally binding contracts. "Confused" and her lover jointly own property, for example, and he may think that signing a mortgage is as great a commitment as marriage. But I've never heard of anyone celebrating the anniversary of their joint mortgage, have you?

Most women—"Confused" included—would prefer a more traditional, romantic symbol of love and commitment than a shared debt. Which is not to say that girls can't be pragmatic. Many view marriage as a prize for being good (in bed, too, they hope). Therefore, they are deeply offended when they have been as good as they know how and aren't given the reward they believe they have earned.

But will he *ever* be ready? I'm asked time and again. Probably, is my best answer. Because men are really more afraid of getting old and stuffy than getting married and making babies, the vast majority of them come to terms with commitment sooner or later—although it might not be soon enough for the girls who love them.

She writes: *"I'm nineteen and I know I've found the man I want to spend the rest of my life with. My boyfriend is twenty. He says he loves me, but he says he's not ready to commit himself. Why is he so immature?"*

I reply: *"He's not immature for his age. He's twenty and smart."*

Judging from all I have observed, every exclusive union has a marrying moment: a peak time, often early on, when the woman's hopes are at their highest and the man's fears are at their lowest. If that unguarded, impetuous moment passes without a proposal, it can be a long wait until the next one. For some couples it never comes again. But if a marrying moment should show up a second time, it will be to a couple who know each other well, see each other clearly, and want each other still. What could serve as a better foundation for a successful marriage than that?

Can You Speed Things Up?

She writes: *"I am twenty-four and have been living with a man for two years. We are deeply attached, but when I mention marriage he says he does not want to give up his bachelor life. What can I do? I don't seem to have any options."*

I reply: *"He is enjoying his life. He has everything he wants, including* you. *Until, and if, he gets a yen for children or suddenly develops an urge for marital stability, he will not change the way things are. Why should he? If you want to make him want to change things, you will have to change first.*

You can (1) go on as you are (sitting tight in a stalled car is *a valid option even if I would not necessarily recommend it); (2) offer him a now-or-never ultimatum and mean it; or (3) leave and see what happens. So, there* are *options, you see. And they are all yours. . . ."*

There are a lot of dangers in waiting around for a man who says he isn't ready to make a commitment. Years, even decades, could slip by while you live on his uncommitted terms and keep hoping he'll change his mind. You could go through sickness and health, poverty and wealth or have babies together and raise

them to maturity before he's ready to marry you.
And he may never be ready. Or, as it sometimes
happens, when he's finally ready to commit himself
it will be to the kid from work he's been seeing on
the sly.

How does a woman make a reluctant man marry
her? I'm not sure I am the right agony aunt to ask.
My feelings about marriage tend to be mannish. But
I'd guess that the only way to lure a man into marriage is to persuade him it would be "more ideal"
than what he already has. And what does he already
have? In the case of "Confused," he has a relatively
happy unlicensed home life. What more does he
need? I'm certain you've heard that gruesome old
wives' stricture against cohabitation: "Why should
a man buy the cow if he gets the milk free?" Well,
repellent as that notion is, I'm afraid it often holds
true even today.

When a man is happy with things as they are, his
lover *could* encourage him to change his mind by
making his life hell on earth. Personally, I find the
idea repugnant and have never actually recommended it, even if there was a chance of its working.
Torture can force all but a saint to recant, but it has
no place between two people who care for each
other.

When I hear about once happy couples who find
their relationship on the rocks right after they marry,
I immediately suspect that one of the pair (not always the woman) must have nagged until the other
begrudgingly agreed to make a commitment in front
of witnesses. And I'm usually right. Twisting arms
and giving ultimatums does more harm to the fabric

of love than either lover realizes, especially if the marriage is undertaken to save an already troubled union. In that case, first comes marriage to help two people get through a rough patch in a love affair, next comes a baby to help them get through trouble in the marriage, and finally comes divorce to put an end to misery and alienation.

(Yes, yes, I know many cohabiting couples marry and are as happy, even happier, than newly wed virgins. However, "Confused" and her lover are in the *other* group, and I am addressing myself to her problem.)

Stalemate!

She writes: *"We've been together for eight years, since I was nineteen. He says he loves me but he doesn't want to marry me or anyone, ever. Should I stay with him? Or would I just be wasting more of my time . . . ?"*

I reply: *"If you really see life with him as a waste of time unless he marries you, then being married means more to you than he does. In other words you are not committed to him. And that's fair enough. But what choice have you? Get out."*

When one lover wants commitment (marriage) and the other hates the whole idea, they have arrived at a perfect stalemate. "If he loved me, he'd marry me," she complains.

"If she loved *me*, she wouldn't ask me to go against my dislike of the whole idea," he retorts.

What does a player do about stalemate? As far as

I can see, if a woman knows she will never be happy without a conventional marriage but finds herself in a longtime love affair with a man who is not amenable, she must decide for herself which matters more to her: living with him and risking being forever "Miss" or leaving him to fulfill herself as another man's "Mrs."

Leaving will be effective only if she leaves to genuinely search for the security, tradition, and stable, sanctioned setting in which to raise children that she is certain she needs. Yes, the man she is leaving *could* come to his senses, follow her, fall on one knee, and offer up the long-awaited diamond ring. But she can't count on that.

There's More to Life Than Marriage

She writes: *"This summer I've been given the chance to travel abroad alone for three to four months. I am twenty-one and have been with my boyfriend for three years. We are happy and want to get married. However, I'm torn between wanting to be with him and taking this wonderful opportunity. He says there is a possibility that we'll split up if I go. How can I decide? I want to have my cake and eat it, which I know isn't possible. . . ."*

I reply: *"Do you know what happens to cake if you don't eat it? It turns green and moldy, dries out, and has to be thrown away. Life's a cake! Enjoy it. How in the world does this man expect a lifelong union with you if he cannot wait even a few short months without threatening a split?*

At your age, if your ambitions are not compatible with those of the man you love and are not supported by him, then my advice must be to scrap the man. There is more than one man for one woman out there, but unsatisfied ambitions never have a second chance."

She writes: *"A year ago I got engaged to my loving and supportive boyfriend of two years. I am twenty, in my last year of college, and he is twenty-eight. When I graduate I want to travel and work abroad, but I also want to be with him. He can't wait until I get a job so we can buy a house. I want this eventually too, but not now. . . ."*

I reply: *"It seems to me that the youth of a liberated woman is better spent in discovery of the world and herself than in service to future security or early commitment. Love and practically everything come more than once in a lifetime. But youth? Honey, this is it. . . ."*

Up to this point, my discussion of the reluctance to make commitments has been somewhat one-sided. The truth is that I wish girls *would* make more original and adventurous use of their youth.

Once upon a time, we were pretty much *born* committed to one way of life over all others. Girls either married a man chosen for them by their parents or undertook conventional spinsterhood, most likely as a caretaker of the very young or the very old. A few lived out socially acceptable variations on the above themes, but none, by and large, had much say in the matter. Only a handful of truly exceptional women managed to reject their prescribed destiny and devoted themselves to art, religion, adventure, commerce, wickedness or some other area of life not ordinarily part of the female inheritance.

Naturally, neither sex was born free from responsibility (or ever will be). Generally, though, men have been confined in a more open prison than women. They were slated to succeed in the family's trade or profession, doing as Daddy had done, only better.

Today, after untold struggle, women finally have the opportunity to commit themselves in as many areas as they have gifts and energy, including to a home and a family, if that is what they choose. Granted, it is still more difficult for a woman to succeed on the wider stages of commerce, politics, arts, and business. But it is a damn sight easier now than ever before, and there are people working to make it easier still. Indeed, the world is not a half bad place to be a woman nowadays. (I for one would not choose to come back as a human male, not until they redesigned the critter, tucked his sex in a safer location, and scaled down his ego to match his capabilities.)

Yet, even though their destinies are no longer pinned to them in the cradle, nine out of ten young women still expect that their sole serious commitment in life will be to a man (and they want a corresponding commitment from him). In fact, not long ago, when an editor asked me to write a piece about young women who were in no hurry for commitment, the few I did come up with were all urban, ambitious career women, many of whom will likely be feeling "unfulfilled" in ten years time and writ-

ing to an agony aunt for advice on where to find
Mister Wonderful.

An ideal marriage remains the ideal way to raise
children, and children are the ultimate commitment.
We cannot return them or exchange them for a better
fit. Women who want children have to adjust their
ambitions and their calendars accordingly, and for
most of us that will always mean marriage. But not
a hasty one, I hope, or one undertaken automatically
as the *only* imaginable commitment, and never as an
excuse to neglect our other commitments—to friendship, work, understanding, our communities, and to
ourselves. I can see the point of marriage being one
commitment among several, but I will never see how
it can be the only commitment in an interesting and
creative life, whether his or hers.

Dear "Confused,"

He engaged himself to you three years ago.
Now he has decided he doesn't want to
marry. Anyone. Ever. And he says not to
take it personally! How does he expect you
to take it, I wonder? It concerns a pretty
personal part of your life, and I hope you've
told him that. I am not saying I think he
should marry you. You've been with him
since you were very, very young (you're still
very, very young), and I wonder if you
aren't a little too keen right now on marrying *him*?

You say you're in a muddle. But at the
same time, you tell me you feel let down,

cheated, not prepared to stick around without commitment. That doesn't sound very muddled to me. He has no intention of committing himself. You have no intention of sticking around without commitment. Where's the muddle? Don't confuse being confused with being reluctant. You're not confused. You just are not eager to leave him, and understandably. It is going to be difficult. But haven't you as good as told me you are going to have to get out and seek commitment somewhere else? What else can you do? I have no magic wand to wave at him and make him change his mind. (And if I *had* a magic wand, I'd be very, very slow ever to use it.)

Commitment is not something anyone can demand from another person. Commitment, it seems to me, is something we seek all our lives to *give*, not to get. When you, and you alone, are committed to what you want, heart and mind and soul, the rest falls into place.

Yours,
Aunt Irma

Agony Aunt's Work Sheet

1. Name six ways a lover shows commitment, starting with the *least* important.

2. Do we have any choice about our own commitments?

3. If "Confused" were committed to her lover, would she care whether or not he married her?

4. Can there be love without commitment?

5. Can there be commitment without love?

6. How far do you think "Confused" or any woman can go to make a reluctant lover marry her without paving the way for resentment and trouble for the future?

7. Would you call time in love wasted if your lover fails to commit himself?

8. If love doesn't last a lifetime, is it love?

9. Write your reply to "Confused."

PROBLEM THREE

• • • • • • • • •

Sex Is Fun.
What's an Orgasm?

Dear Irma,

I don't think I've ever had an orgasm. I've always enjoyed sex, so it hasn't really bothered me before. But now I'm with a guy I really care for, and he is starting to get upset. He says all his other girlfriends always had orgasms, and it makes him feel inadequate when I don't. Please help.

"Non-O"

If Queen Victoria ever had orgasms, she kept mum about it. Freud didn't see any real need for women to have them. And lots of feminists thought the vaginal orgasm was a myth created by men, presumably to make us worry about ourselves. It's only within living memory that women have been given the impression that they're *supposed* to have orgasms. Before that, we had beaux, lovers, husbands. We had babies and headaches and sometimes even a good time. But orgasms? Not so you'd talk about them, thank you.

Then in the seventies, about the same time I started writing "The Agony Column," it seemed as if every third letter dealt with orgasms, and two out of three of those were complaints from women who had never had one. Words like "nonorgasmic" and the perfectly disgusting "sexually dysfunctional" appeared overnight, replacing the term previously used to describe a female incapable of arousal: "frigid."

Sexual problems continue to pour into "The Agony Column" of course, but those specifically concerned with an inability to achieve climax are down to about two in ten. Does the decrease mean there has been an increase in orgasmic women over recent years? I cannot say for sure. My guess is that two decades of emphasis on sex in the media as well as the widespread attention given to the clitoris and G spots has managed to remove the ignorance and inhibitions that prevented women of other generations from having orgasms—or even admitting they knew what they were.

That is, for the most part, a good thing. In a world as rich in choices as ours, everything we accept means rejecting other things. For every gain, we suffer losses. . . .

She writes: *"My boyfriend and I have tried all sorts of positions and games. Sometimes I 'come' during foreplay, but I have never been able to orgasm with him inside me. He doesn't know, and I don't want him to worry about it because I love him very much and our lovemaking is wonderful for me, even when I don't have an orgasm. Do I have a problem?''*

I reply: *"You must have a problem. Only people with problems write to agony aunts. . . .''*

A lot of girls who fail to have orgasms regularly say they adore sex anyway. Men find that hard to believe, and I did too during my pioneering days. But now I wonder. Maybe women *can* enjoy sexual fulfillment without obligatory orgasms. Perhaps it wasn't so smart to isolate orgasm from the erotic whole and put it at the level of a punchline without which there is no story.

A clinical element has crept into our sexual encounters. Lovemaking has become less meandering and feminine, more aggressive, mannish, and goal oriented, as if making love were a competitive sport rather than one of the few remaining activities in life where warmth, softness, and tenderness count.

Back in the bad old days I sometimes advised women who were going crazy trying to have orgasms to have something else instead: a rollicking good time in bed, for instance, fun in the bath, passion, affection, comfort, and fidelity. Now that more women seem to be able to climax all over the place (or so they tell me), I find myself advising them not to *forget* all those other good things while they're at it.

What Is an Orgasm Anyway?

She writes: *"Dear Irma, I have multiple orgasms almost every time my boyfriend and I make love.*

Seven was my highest. This is not the sort of topic to bring up at a dinner party, so I do not know for sure if it is exceptional. . . .''

I reply: *''Come again? I didn't quite catch what's bothering you . . . ?''*

Once men found their way to the clitoris, developed staying power, and started to catch on to female orgasms, it became apparent that some women have orgasms every time (and sometimes more than once). Many women have orgasms most of the time. Most women have orgasms some of the time. And some women never have orgasms at all—in more than a few instances, because they do not know how.

Women who do not know how to have orgasms have never masturbated, I guess. Or if they have, it must have been with a singular lack of enthusiasm. A few who have written to me obviously confuse approaching orgasm with an urge to urinate and so stop themselves short of the top, perhaps to spare the sheets (though clean sheets have never been a gauge of good sex).

''What is sex like?'' I asked an older more experienced girl when I was about ten.

''Very sticky,'' she replied.

And as far as it went, that turned out to be an accurate and vivid description.

I wonder if ''Non-O'' masturbates? In the seventies and eighties, defending masturbation was such an important part of an agony aunt's job that my accountant was only half joking when he suggested I ask vibrator manufacturers for a commission. I'm surprised self-pleasuring still needs to be advocated in this enlightened day and age, but "Non-O" may have slipped through the net. If she *had* masturbated she could not say she doesn't *think* she has ever reached orgasm. One way or another, she would know.

She writes: *"I am twenty . . . I masturbate . . . not every day, but it makes me feel dirty and unclean. Whenever I do, something bad happens . . . I get into bad debt, I fight with my boyfriend or my mom. I try to stop, but in two or three months I do it again . . . I feel guilty and ashamed and the bad luck starts. How can I kick the habit?"*

I reply: *"There is nothing intrinsically wrong with masturbation. It does not harm anyone. It does not cheat anyone. It does not cause acne, madness, blindness, baldness or 'runs of bad luck'. . . . not unless you decide to punish yourself for your pleasure."*

Masturbation is one way for any woman to experience the sensation of orgasm and learn the best way to arrive at it. Then, she can tell her lover how to get her to a climax—if she is bold enough. I used to recommend talking frankly in bed, but I now think that talking dirty is probably more effective and certainly sexier.

I suspect few young women are so straightforward or unromantic about sex as to put their preferences to a lover in so many words. An easier plan, and much more fun, is to steer him in the right direction by sounds of pleasure. Then, when he's getting it right, try that classic phrase: "Don't stop."

Faking It

In the past, letter writers used to say, "I've never had an orgasm and it makes me feel disappointed and inadequate. . . ." Now, they are more likely to say, "I don't have orgasms, and it makes *my lover* feel disappointed and inadequate." Is that progress or is that progress?

Yes, I guess it probably *is* progress. In the old days, whenever a woman didn't have an orgasm, she faked one. Why? To make *him* "feel good about himself."

God only knows how many women routinely fake orgasms. Honest women, women who would not dream of lying to their lovers on any other score, women who would swear under oath that they believed truth and mutual trust to be the linchpin of a solid union have been known to put on performances worthy of Academy Awards. Why do they go to such lengths to make a man feel good about himself? Because they are afraid if they don't, he will find someone else who moans, "Oooooh, aaaah, you're the greatest!"—even if she is lying through her teeth.

If men could fake orgasms as easily as women, they probably would, at least occasionally (when they have a meeting in the morning, for instance, and the alarm clock is set to go off at 6 A.M.).

Faking, in and of itself, is neither "good" nor "bad." The real trouble is that lying about anything tends to box the liar into a lonely corner where the truth becomes increasingly difficult *ever* to reveal.

What *does* a woman who has routinely faked orgasms do if she decides she wants the real thing? Casually mention that her operatic efforts to persuade him of his manliness and incomparable sexual prowess were all a sham? At least ''Non-O'' is upfront about not having orgasms—even if her motives for wanting to have them are the same as the orgasm faker's: to make *him* happy.

Orgasms Aren't Everything

For good and for ill, the biggest difference between the sexes is sex. As a general rule, women take longer to get aroused than men, and their excitement is not so localized. They can't always be as spontaneous about sex, either. Like it or not, women's biology (and a little thing called fertility) means every lovemaking session has the potential to be a big production number for them.

Men, on the other hand, have a tendency to aim for a goal in a way women have not quite achieved yet and probably never will. (Actually, I hope we don't, and I have faith that women are too smart and too busy to ever see scoring points as anything more than an amusement.)

Even though the classic wham-bam quickie is tolerated by women who write to me, only anal intercourse is less popular. Orgasm may be the high point of lovemaking, but most women also revel in all that happens before it—and continue to complain of the absence of caresses afterward.

Ironically, one of the best ways for a woman to achieve her elusive orgasm is to stop consciously chasing it. Sex is playful. Sex is fun. Sex is sexy. But when everything in you is screaming, "Will I? Won't I?," sex is a chore and boring.

To get out of that rut, "Non-O" might ask her lover to spend a night or a weekend being erotic without penetration. Tender, patient, and attentive touching, massaging, and caressing (not to mention fantasies, role-playing, and sex toys) that make orgasm the equivalent of an after-dinner mint are likely to serve up that confection to any woman who has never had one before or who has a lot of trouble on that score.

Since sensuality for its own sake is a somewhat alien concept for men, a woman may have to orchestrate the more silken, sensual aspects of love-making until her lover gets the hang of it.

Of course, no man can be *that* tender, patient, and attentive every time, nor every woman always in the mood for that approach. But it isn't a bad idea to periodically schedule time to wallow in erotic pleasure. A friend of mine and her lover call these sessions "parties we both attend, but nobody has to come."

Men, Women, and Sexual Problems

She writes: *"We used to make love all the time. Now I'm lucky if it's once a month. When I complain, he says he's satisfied and what's my problem?"*

It's a bother, isn't it, that ego is the primary male sex organ? It means every sexual encounter for a man is to some degree a challenge. Any problem or shade of criticism whatsoever is a blow first to his ego, then to his erection. For every complaint I receive from a woman who has trouble having orgasms, two arrive from women whose lovers get there too fast and three more from women whose men have practically stopped trying.

As things stand (or not), problems in the sex department scream "failure" at a man, and because men are competitive by training and nature, failure hits them hard (especially when they are failing at something they hear their buddies boasting about doing perfectly). That's why the average man calls any sexual complaint *your* problem. But the truth is that if one partner has a problem with what is (or isn't) going on sexually, the other one automatically does too.

If a man is a lousy lover, or hardly a lover at all, a woman is faced with the daunting task of getting him to discuss a problem he does not realize or want to admit exists. Whining, shouting, and screaming won't work. He'll either retreat into silence or down to the bar. Bullying and threatening to seek satisfaction elsewhere have no place between two people with feelings for each other. And casting blame will only inflict pain and put him on the defensive, which in the end is about as helpful as casting stones.

Don't ever fool yourself into thinking that men have no feelings. They feel pain too, believe me, but they see it as a weakness in themselves and have trouble expressing it except as anger. Thus, the most courteous and effective way to approach your mate on the subject of sex is with tact, gentleness, and seduction. Wouldn't you have him approach *you* that way if the shoe were on the other foot (as it sometimes is)? Always go into an encounter of this nature fully prepared, with all arguments marshaled and the number of a counselor to call if he agrees to see one with you.

As areas of contention between couples go, sexual problems tend to respond easily, even pleasantly, to counseling. However, if he refuses to change his style or seek advice, then you will have to decide what you really need from the sexual side of your relationship, what you're willing to do without, and how far you are willing to go to get what you want.

It may be necessary to separate temporarily. This would certainly show you mean business. Moreover, time and space apart would give you both a chance to cool down, gain perspective, and decide whether you can reconcile as lovers, friends, or neither. Of course, you could move in opposite directions while you're apart, in which case, your temporary separation could become a permanent estrangement. He might go off with someone else. Or you might. And that's why leaving is a gamble.

The only people who can afford to gamble are those who can afford to lose. If you feel these stakes are too high, you will have to look for another equally persuasive but less risky way to convince your man to take your mutual sexual problem seriously. A vengeful infidelity to get even with him for his insensitivity is *not* a good idea, by the by. And nagging, tears, and long silences are ineffective and as hard on you as they are on him. They quickly become habits—the kind that destroy entire relationships.

Then again, you could decide to live with a less than ideal sex life. Surrendering to the way things are isn't such a horrible option, especially if you're satisfied with other aspects of your relationship (or terrified of losing your man). To be quite honest, there are more important things to achieve in this life than orgasms—although I still hope "Non-O" and other young women like her someday get a chance to experience them.

Dear "Non-O,"

Orgasm isn't a goal, true love, or the holy grail. Orgasms are delirious fun. And what you are after is *fun*. Don't chase after it. Let it catch you. First off, however, you'd better make sure you know what it is. Orgasm is also called "climax" because that describes it precisely. It's a release of sexual excitement, a few moments when mind and body explode like fireworks. If you see lovemaking as a series of peaks, orgasm is the one that goes off the scale. Once an orgasm is underway, it is out of control, which, I believe, is the very reason some women fear it.

I'm sure you've felt excitement, all alone, from accidental or deliberate self-stimulation. You would be wise to set out deliberately to masturbate beyond the point where you've stopped previously. If you are uninhibited enough, your boyfriend could give you a hand, as it were. Otherwise, do it alone. Let your thoughts loose and continue

all the way to climax. You will know it when it happens because nothing much more *can* happen. Some women have multiple orgasms. But I have been a believer all my life in quality, not quantity, and I do not envy them. Once you have found your way to your own climax, there is no reason to envy anyone.

As soon as you're sure you know exactly the sensation you are after, you and your boyfriend can go in pursuit of it as often as you both wish. Slowly, slowly wins this race, remember. As a matter of fact, why don't you put aside one night to make endless love, having decided beforehand *not* to let an orgasm stop you or come between you. That will show you what levels of excitement you can achieve. It also relieves you of the need to take orgasm so damned seriously that it preempts love, closeness, delight, and pleasure in each other's bodies.

And while we're talking pleasure, oral sex (by him) is a well-traveled and practically irresistible route to orgasm. I wonder if either of you has an insurmountable bias against it? If so, a scented bath (together?) could ease inhibitions and a bedside jar of honey, though it adds calories and is hell on the sheets, has been known to work a treat.

Cheerfully,
Aunt Irma

Agony Aunt's Work Sheet

1. Name six things sex is for.

2. Can you imagine a man and woman in love who do not make love? Under what circumstances?

3. If a woman does not have an orgasm, do you think: (a) she has failed, (b) he has failed, (c) love has failed, or (d) nothing and nobody have failed?

4. Is faking an orgasm the same as lying? Why or why not? ·

5. What are the qualities of a great lover's technique, starting with the *least* important?

6. Think of three things "Non O" might do to make her lover sexier?

7. Write your own answer to her letter.

PROBLEM FOUR

• • • • • • • • •

Can There Be
Love Without Trouble?

Dear Irma,

My boyfriend and I have been living together for nearly two years, and we knew
each other for a year before that. I'm
twenty-three. He's twenty-nine. In the beginning our sex life was great. Then it tapered
off. Now we make love maybe once a week.
Twice, if I'm lucky, and it's all over in
minutes. He's just started his own business,
and I know he's worried about it so I try not
to push. But the other day when I was looking through his desk I found a girlie magazine. Also, I found a porn video in his old
suitcase at the back of a closet. The thought
of him looking at that stuff makes me sick.
Why can't I be all he needs? Please help me.
I'm so unhappy.

"In Pain"

"In Pain's" letter reminds me of a time many, many years ago when I was down and out in London and went to work for a small publicity agency. One Monday morning, our main client decided to stop being merely the proprietor of a few clubs and to become the Hugh Heffner of Great Britain instead. By Tuesday I found myself on the editorial board of the first English-language girlie magazine to be produced outside the United States.

Our biggest problem, as it turned out, was not finding women ready to strip for the camera but discouraging those who really shouldn't. Droves of them applied. We looked at photographs of naked housewives, naked secretaries, and naked bank clerks, as well as professional models and strippers.

My picks—generally gals with bones, strong lines, and faces ready to spit in a man's eye at twenty paces—were usually vetoed by my male bosses, and in a short time I started to see why. What they were looking for in their stroke maidens was an air of unquestioning acquiescence.

"These aren't supposed to be *real* women," one of the senior editors explained. "They're sexual icons." *And when it comes to sexual icons, love does not enter the picture.* Men in search of fantasy thrills mostly want a tootsie who advertises availability. They mainly go for images of eager, uncritical complicity: a face and posture that says, "Whatever you want, I want it just as much." Men see the porn queen as a female they can get the hots for, fuck, satisfy, and then happily, guiltlessly leave just by turning the page. She poses much less of a threat to loving, monogamous relationships than the young women who write to me seem to think.

Yes, pornography can be found under the beds of rapists and mass murderers. But if you were to look, you also would find it under the beds of lawyers, judges, policemen, and other pillars of society. Indeed, for every woman who poses in a dirty magazine or wiggles around in a porno video, there are hundreds, even thousands of men who will get off just looking at her. If porn demeans anyone—and I am not persuaded it does—then statistically, it demeans mostly men.

I find it thought provoking, incidentally, that the majority of women who write to "The Agony Column" about their lovers' porn rarely complain that it demeans women by presenting them as sex objects. Instead, they are hurt because the charmers in porn magazines make them feel like less adequate sex objects themselves.

Does Love Mean Never Having to Look at Pornography?

She writes: *"My boyfriend and I have been together for nearly three years. Recently I found out that he bought ten pornographic magazines from my brother. They had agreed not to tell me. My boyfriend told me it was just a stage guys go through, but we are both very sexually active. Ever since I found out, I've been miserable. I cry my eyes out, feeling so stupid, like I didn't please him. How could my own brother do that to me?"*

I reply: *"He did not think it mattered. To be honest, neither do I. But as it matters to you, it's something you'll have to talk to your boyfriend about and thrash out together, until you are both happy with the solution. . . ."*

A man I know claims that men's susceptibility to the visual image (which he calls "the flash mechanism") is as instinctive as the quickened heartbeat of a hunter when his prey leaps into sight. Any heterosexual male free from trauma or inhibition enjoys looking at an attractive female body, my friend maintains. And *any* attractive female body will do.

When a guy is down, a glimpse of flesh lifts his spirits. When he's fretful, it soothes him. And when he is in danger it reminds him that bodies were not given merely so we could dispatch them to kingdom come.

It isn't personal, my friend notes. Soldiers in a war zone don't care any less for their girlfriends and wives at home just because there are nudie pinups spread-eagled over their bunks.

Pornographic magazines are made for masturbation, and in most men's minds masturbation is a sex act altogether apart from love. The moving image on the screen, a voice talking dirty, or a photograph kick-starts erections, release, and a time between the two when all other concerns can be forgotten. In that sense, a man's indulgence in pornography, especially during stressful moments in his life, is comparable to a common practice among stressed out women—soothing themselves with a trip to the refrigerator for a solitary "go" at the chocolate ice cream.

When a man reaches for a girlie magazine or dials

a phone sex line, he knows he won't have to worry about failing to maintain an erection or satisfy a sexual partner. "Porn is uncomplicated," said a chum I consult on such issues. "And life is hard. I'm crazy about my girlfriend. But sometimes I want to indulge my sex drive without a thought to love, caring, or someone else's enjoyment."

What's more, for every young man who jerks off over an airbrushed image there is a girl building erotic fantasies around the sugary goo of a paperback bodice ripper. Beyond the fact that men find pictures sexually stimulating while women are more responsive to the wistful allure of words, is there really so much difference between the two? Only that men usually forget their dreamboats moments after they climax, while plenty of girls never abandon their romantic daydreams completely (and least of all when they are in the arms of a flesh-and-blood lover).

She writes: *"Dear Irma, I'm horribly worried that I am being unfaithful to my boyfriend because I think of Keanu Reeves whenever he touches me. . . ."*

I reply: *"You are no more being unfaithful to your boyfriend than you are being unfaithful to Keanu Reeves. . . . "*

It is my impression that Misses April, May, June, and July are interchangeable as far as men are concerned. Their porn princesses are a lot less real to them than a movie star was to this young woman (and many others like her). I've actually had *Cosmo* readers ask me how to find their idol's address because they "just know" they are meant for each other.

Admittedly, this movie-star phenomenon is not

yet as widespread among adult females as porn is among young adult males. (Most men outgrow pornography as they age and their sexual urges become mature; not to mention "less.") But the fantasies of starstruck women who confuse carnal desire with love tend to be solitary turn-ons. (What man will be aroused by imagining he's Keanu Reeves while caressing his girlfriend?) Pornography, on the other hand, can sometimes be shared. Plenty of women find some varieties of it titillating too. Watching films together, even shopping for them, has been known to add zip to a flagging sex life.

But Porn Does Have a Down Side

When I fail to attack pornography wholesale, I get a very angry response from readers. But I genuinely believe that pornography in general does our society infinitely less harm than crackpot cults, pseudo-therapies, racist doctrine, Barbie-doll role models for little girls, soap opera ethics, most television talk shows, and a whole lot more schlock we tolerate and defend.

Pornography has been with us since the Romans and before, but recently it has become a political issue. And that means we have to race to a "pro" or "anti" position, sign petitions, and cease to debate the subject or treat it with an open mind. Seesaw polemics of this nature do not advance anything but trouble. By forcing us to choose a side, they put a moratorium on weighing evidence. By presenting topics as "good" or "bad," they turn discussion into personal abuse and prevent us from acknowledging matters of degree.

Naturally, there is porn and there is porn. When it involves those who have been recruited at too young an age to know what they are doing or when it is sold in places where it is inappropriate and offensive, then the community at large has every right to object, as they do to the sale of alcohol.

Yet, all in all, fantasies are not deeds, and masturbation does not harm other human beings. If a man's habits do not affect his primary sexual relationship, they are nobody's business but his own. Which is not to say that all men do beastly things—or that women ought to tolerate anything a man's brutish nature drives him to do.

While I will continue to defend porn in general, I must acknowledge that problems with it do exist. If "In Pain's" lover uses looking at girlie magazines and masturbating to replace sexual contact with her, then they have a problem. In addition, when two people are in love and living together, it is the utmost discourtesy for one of them to use or display in their common space *any* material that genuinely offends or repulses the other.

By the same token, however, roommates and lovers also need areas of privacy—a desk drawer, for instance, or an "old suitcase at the back of a closet"—where the other never intrudes.

Thus, if "In Pain" is truly repulsed by her boyfriend's girlie magazines, common courtesy requires him to keep them out of sight and "In Pain" to keep her nose out of his probable hiding places. As my old mother says, "She who peeks through keyholes never sees anything very nice."

And You Thought Porn Was a Problem?!

She writes: *"One day last month I came home early from work and found my boyfriend in our bedroom dressed up in my clothes. He said he was curious about how it felt. But I think there is more to it than that. We've always had a good sex life. Why is he doing this to me? Is he gay?"*

For a lot of women it isn't particularly difficult to accept a man's penchant for porn without a trace of "In Pains's" distress. I know I'd rather see my man have his wicked way and turn the page than bed my friends or have sex with prostitutes, especially without benefit of condoms. But could I happily make love with a cross-dresser? Who knows? My ability to do so has never been tested.

I do know that few women who write to me are quite as perplexed as those who discover that the man they live with is a transvestite or has some other sexual secret. The first thing I do is try to clear up their confusion.

The behavior they've stumbled upon may shock or disgust them, I explain, but it isn't something their lover or husband is doing *to* them. It is something he is driven to do by deep urges of his own. He has probably been too ashamed and frightened to discuss this side of himself with *anyone*. I also assure them that cross-dressing is a separate issue from homosexuality.

Transvestites are not always gay. And the source of their preference has not been explained conclusively—although it could have its roots in an early sensual encounter with silks. Whatever the cause, transvestites get a sexual thrill from being done up in our gear. But that does not mean they also share our preference for male sexual partners. (Actually, I have a hunch that the sexual orientation attached to cross-dressing is not homosexuality so much as male masochism. But then, I *would* think that, as I've always found high heels perfectly agonizing to wear.)

I have heard from women who say they have come to enjoy helping their lovers dress, shop, and get made up. Although some of their letters land on my desk with the unmistakable *thunk* of phonies written by men to excite themselves, I certainly wouldn't dismiss all of them as untruths. As for the partners of transvestites who aren't so accommodating, they have a great support system I feel happy to recommend.

What About . . . ?

She writes: *"Last night when I was getting into the shower, I heard a noise. I looked out to see a figure on the roof. Suddenly, I had the sick realization it was my husband. He tried to deny it but admitted he was trying to spy on me and had done so before. I was numb with horror. He says it's because I never let him see my body. . . ."*

I reply: *"Why not find ways to incorporate 'peeping' into your sex life sometimes? Don't quite close*

the door when you bathe ... undress in front a mir-
ror strategically placed. ... There's no law against
it in your own home. It will become a problem, how-
ever, if he is driven out into the neighborhood to
indulge his yen. ..."

Bondage. Spanking. Peeping at your lover in your own home. Fantasies of rape. In my view, there's nothing "wrong" with any of it. Silk scarves and handcuffs are longtime sex toys, nineteenth century lords and ladies spanked, and fantasies are fanta-sies—not facts. A shared taste for some spicy sa-domasochism is not bad, bad, bad. Like shaving pubic hair or sex in the great out-of-doors, bondage and a bit of frisky slap and tickle can be fun, fun, fun.

However, any special sexual activity can cease to be part of a playful repertoire and instead become obsessional. How can you tell when that line's been crossed? For starters, an obsessional sexual activity tends to satisfy only one partner, although the other partner may "play along" because she fears she'll be dumped if she doesn't. Second, an obsessional sexual scenario often comes between lovers and love, keeping them from being truly intimate.

For instance, a woman I've known for many years was so deeply attracted to sadistic sex (on rather a cheerful level involving "naughty girls" and so forth), she could not enjoy herself without a slipper or paddle nearby. She thought this was fine. Every-body willing. Nobody hurt. And with the peculiarly naive egocentricity of people who have special sex-ual tastes, she assumed that anyone who tried it would agree that no sexual encounter was complete without some amicable slapping around.

Inevitably, she attracted a series of men who wanted to play her game, but not one of her partners lasted much more than a year or two. And not one of them moved on to a happy relationship afterward. Although it ended in orgasm all around, my friend's compulsion to act out whenever she made love ultimately destroyed her chances for a lasting affair or marriage. What looked like an erotic game was actually a symptom of a central condition suitable for treatment.

Two's Company—Three's Trouble

She writes: *"We've been together for nearly two years. Our sex life has been good. Now he says he'd like to bring another woman into the scene. He says it's up to me. The idea turns me on. But I'm scared to ruin what we have. Should I do it?"*

Lately, letters like this one have been arriving with increasing frequency, and it seems to me that the interest in threesomes is becoming a fad, one I'm not inclined to encourage. Whenever I receive a three-in-a-bed question, my impulse is against it. Because, yes, there are limits to what is sane and healthy, even in the name of love.

Modern lovemaking is pretty much detached from reproduction. It's sought after for more than affection and pleasure. People make love out of vanity, loneliness, sometimes a thirst for power. When a lover brings a third person into bed, it is *always* a power trip. He wants to see how enslaved and obe-

dient his woman is. It is her acquiescence, her buck-
ling under to his coercion, and the depths to which
she will go to accommodate him that turn him on.
And I cannot in good faith endorse that sort of rit-
ualized humiliation as an expression of love.

If I am revealing a prejudice after railing against
them, so be it. Knowing our prejudices and replacing
them with understanding is a lifetime job that I can
safely say I have not finished. Besides, a few prejudices are backed up by enough practical evidence
to relieve us of the need to struggle too hard against
them—and my opposition to threesomes fits that
bill.

She writes: *"He says if I love him, I'll let him
bring another woman into our lovemaking. . . ."*

I reply: *"If he loved anyone other than himself he
would not resort to blackmail. It takes two to make
blackmail complete, by the way: perpetrator and victim."*

I'm rarely swayed by a young woman's assurances that "the idea turns me on a little. . . ." So
what if it does? Fantasies are a turn-on, and some
can be fun to enact. But those involving people other
than the central couple are better left to the imagination. In the hard, solid world threesomes are ac-
companied by jealousy and other dangers—
including the fact that, in becoming real, fantasies
tend to lose their power and must constantly be
stoked to higher heat. Thus, once you agree to a
threesome, there is no saying "no" next time, no
going back, only forward into greater deterioration
of privacy, intimacy, and trust.

Love *can* stretch to incredible dimensions with

less trouble than most of us imagine, especially if we set aside our knee-jerk prejudices and rely on our intellects as well as our emotions. Yet, in the end, there is only so much trouble love can contain without causing us unbearable pain and only so much understanding and loving acceptance we can muster before descending into self-abasement, degradation, and despair. A woman who wants to survive intact knows when a troubled love affair is pushing against the boundaries set by self-respect and self-preservation. And she gets out fast before her emotions are engaged in a lost cause or enslaved to a dream of what is dead and gone.

But I Love Him . . .

She writes: *"He never speaks to me except about what he wants to eat. We don't have sex anymore. Sometimes he doesn't come home at night. But I love him. Don't tell me to leave him. . . ."*

"But I love him" are words that depress my spirits. I've heard: "He beats me, *but I love him,*" "he cheats on me, *but I love him,*" "he gambles away our rent money, *but I love him,*" and once, "I came home and found him in bed with my mother, *but I love him.*"

Leave the plaintive, long-suffering "but I love him" to the old-fashioned torch singers, I say. As a reason for staying in a despicable situation, that phrase is unsuitable to our time and an insult to our emergent feminine pride.

Practically without exception when "but I love

him'' letters come my way, they include the stipulation: ''Don't tell me to leave him.'' Well, my friends, I'm afraid that in some cases leaving him is the smart thing, in fact, the only thing, to do. What is the alternative? To nag, scream, cry, beg, suffer? To make love synonymous with pain and then pass the entire masochistic mess on to yet another generation? Think it over.

More Trouble

We think about sex all the time, but not much beyond how much we want it. That's why it is such a perplexing area of life. In the throes of sexual excitement, we rarely consider the possible consequences of our actions.

She writes: *''While on holiday I met a man I liked a lot, and I slept with him. He used a condom. Now I can't eat or sleep, I'm so terrified I might have caught AIDS. I would never have slept with someone so casually here.''*

I reply: *''AIDS is not a punishment. AIDS is not retribution. AIDS is a sexually transmitted disease, and it must be approached as civilized people approach any disease. The chances of your having contracted AIDS from your liaison are very, very small. To set your mind at ease, go to your local VD clinic and have a simple blood test. A physical fact can be faced. It is superstition, guilt, and panic that put us to shame.''*

These days all I need to do is suggest to a grown woman that she forgive her husband his infidelity or forgive herself her own, and a torrent of letters take me to task for neglecting to mention what unforgivable selfishness it is to risk contracting and passing on HIV, the virus that causes AIDS. Well, the danger certainly exists, and it's a virulent danger. But the risk of contracting HIV can be reduced by using condoms—which means it's not dangerous enough to eliminate infidelity, promiscuity, or alcoholic one-night stands. We still need to think about these issues and understand the human emotions involved.

If moralizers had their way, "safe sex" would be a euphemism for no sex at all. But are we going to put a virus in charge of human passion and charity? Are we going to substitute a disease for our conscience?

Moderation and common sense must surely be a more progressive, humane, and far-sighted defense against illness than hysterical fulminations from the legion who can hardly wait to shout "I told you so!"

Borrowing Trouble

She writes: "*My boyfriend is twenty-three, and last week he had an erection in his sleep. How do I know he was dreaming of me? He says he can't remember. It's driving me crazy. . . .*"

Cries from the heart like this one arrive on my desk so often that I'm starting to think women will confuse *anything* the slightest bit sexy with love itself.

I reply: "*Give the guy a break. Maybe he was dreaming of you. Maybe he was dreaming of Hilary*

Clinton or the queen. Maybe he was dreaming of winning the lottery. Maybe he wasn't dreaming at all. Young men's cocks have dreams of their own. Erections happen. They are a physical response, not a barometer of emotions. No matter how deep love is there are areas it cannot penetrate. It may encourage erections, but it can hardly prevent one, especially in a man who is sound asleep.''

She writes: *''While cleaning out a boxful of junk in his bookcase, I found poems he had written about a former girlfriend. We've been together for nearly a year now. They'd broken up a year before we met. He swore to me it was all finished with her. But why would he keep these poems if he didn't still think about her? I'm so hurt and angry. . . .''*

I reply: *''He keeps the poems not because he remembers her (though of course he* does, *as I hope you remember every man who touched you deeply). He keeps the poems because he remembers* himself *as the kind of young lover who wrote poems. He's secretly proud of his poems, and even though he probably would not be awfully pleased to know you have been snooping through his things, I'll bet he'd like you to appreciate his romantic soul. So instead of attacking him about his 'ex,' try talking to him about poetry. Better still, write* him *a poem. Play your cards right, in other words, and when he feels encouraged to write poems again, they will be for you.''*

She writes: *''I love him very much but I don't think we're compatible. We live together. I love to shop on my days off, but he always wants to mooch around the house fixing things or go out to a football game with his buddies. He is being insensitive to my needs. . . . I don't want to go on this way.''*

I reply: *"A bonus for little boys becoming big boys is that they no longer have to go shopping with Mommy. You sound to me like a little girl trying to play house with a boy who'd rather not play. But this is not a game; it's the real thing. And if a grown man doesn't want to shop, for goodness sakes, why should he? Shop alone, and be happy the broken lamp is fixed when you get home. (Otherwise, go ahead and break up, with my congratulations for having put forward the silliest reason I've come across.)"*

You name it, and somewhere, somehow, it is causing someone trouble in love. Much of this misery is self-inflicted, brought on by overblown notions, which simultaneously exaggerate what most of us believe love *should* be and underestimate the moving, human, wild, bemusing, relevant, sheltering, accepting thing love *can* be.

Love is never exactly what you want it to be. It's what you get—if you're lucky. Trouble comes when you think your love *should* be other than he is.

"Love is not love," said the man who knew it all, "Which alters when it alteration finds. . . ."

When I started being an agony aunt, my impulse was to assume all flea bites were symptoms of a deeper malaise. He didn't want to shop, for example, because he resented her spending money he had earned or money she had earned, et cetera, et cetera. Occasionally I was correct. Sometimes quibbles *were* the surface eruptions of something big, bad, and deep. But I have since discovered that they just as often express nothing more than the immaturity of the writer, her exaggerated idea of what a man *should* be, her foggy vision of who the man in hand *is*, and her unreadiness for the give-and-take of live-in love.

Wedding Woes

She writes: *"My boyfriend and I are planning our wedding. Both my parents are elderly, and my father had a heart attack a few years ago. He can't sleep at the thought of having to make a speech, so how will he cope on the actual day? I am getting very stressed about this. My boyfriend doesn't seem at all concerned. Am I making a mistake?"*

I reply: *"Weddings are a celebration, not a drama. Just because the bride's father usually makes a speech does not mean the rule is carved in stone. Someone else—uncle or friend—could explain your father's allergy to public speaking and propose a toast. Don't turn your wedding day into a test. . . ."*

The list of wedding worries is as long as a society guest list. His mother drinks, for instance, and could make a scene at the reception. Her best friend's boyfriend doesn't like her brother, and so she won't be a bridesmaid. His family *should* butt out because her family is paying—and if her husband-to-be really loved her, he'd take her side.

"Call the whole thing off, then, or elope," is the response that arises in me without fail. Why question love itself because of some point of protocol?

A wedding is to marriage as a funeral is to death,

only a wedding happens to precede the greater event. (When I was a younger, I preferred funerals because nobody pointed to an open grave and said, "Irma, you'll be next!") And weddings are the *only* general area of complaint for which I have never received one single solitary letter from a man. I imagine that's because a man wouldn't write, "My wedding is the most important day of my life . . ." and women inevitably do.

If her wedding really is the most important day she can look back upon or foresee, then she has not lived well enough or long enough to know what she is talking about. Moreover, her use of the pronoun "my," ("*my* wedding," "*my* life," never "*our*") stands as evidence of her ignorance of what lies ahead: *marriage*, for crying out loud!

Why don't we do away with weddings once and for all? In the end, they're too cute, too geared for women only, too reminiscent of the dowry system and daddy's-little-girlishness. Down with them! What do you say? A dignified ceremony in plain clothes with a glass of champagne and a few dollars donated to start the couple on their way is surely all anyone needs to begin a happy marriage.

When Love Is Blind and Then Some

She writes: "*I married my husband six months ago. We had known each other ten months before that. He never gets out of bed. He cannot work. He had an illness before I met him and needs to take all kinds of medication. The pills make him sick all the time. His doctors say they are not sure he will ever improve. I work day and night to keep us going. I'm still young, and I want to leave him so I can have some kind of life. But how will he get along without me?''*

Where were these two during their courtship—on separate planets? His illnesses are not new. His inability to work could not have started on their honeymoon. Was she so dazzled by love and the idea of marriage that the effects of his medications were not evident to her soon after they met?

We marry for better or for worse, which is all the more reason to have a pretty good idea of what we're getting into *before* we make that commitment. Yet, an alarming number of women are genuinely surprised to find themselves hitched to inveterate gamblers, junkies, lechers, or drunks, even though the signs were in front of their eyes long before the wedding. Were they too befuddled by emotion to notice, or did they imagine he'd change once they got him over the altar and home for keeps?

Sure, some men deliberately hide their flaws or embellish their attributes. So do women. As a matter of course, couples in love try to show (and tend to see) only their good sides. And, yes, there are conmen who knowingly deceive girls for their own nefarious ends, but certainly not as many as there are girls who tell me they married without any idea their new husbands had been in prison or were bankrupt or had fathered an illegitimate child. Others wed the Romeo they met on vacation based on nothing more than his big brown eyes and their own adolescent daydreams.

Love is blind, to be sure, and blinding, deaf, and deafening. I know love drives us crazy. But must it also make us stupid?

Women in particular have an allergic reaction to romance. One whiff of love induces such stupefied lunacy that it would be foolhardy to open a corner shop much less enter into a lifelong contract and start producing a whole new line of human beings. That's why, when I rule the world, I'm going to push through a law that allows couples in love to make love until the cows come home, but forbids them to marry, have a child, or commit themselves to any binding agreement until their romantic and sexual passions have subsided a bit and been tempered by acceptance and understanding.

In the world I ruled, no woman would ever again join forces with a man because she felt she could not live without him. They'd move in together only when she was sure she could live *with* him. It's a nice idea, and it would certainly ease us agony aunts into early retirement.

Oh, Those Ex-wives and Stepchildren!

She writes: *"His ex-wife is on the phone every week asking him to do things like pick the kids up after school. She even called him once to change a light-bulb. They were married for fifteen years. Can't she understand he's with me now?"*

I reply: *"She was his dependent for fifteen years. And she never asked for her freedom, did she? Independence is bound to be hard and find her utterly*

unprepared. Be patient. And be warned by her ex-
ample not to let yourself become so totally dependent
you are helpless on your own.''

Any man who has been married and divorced has
an ex-wife. And to whatever degree she still intrudes
upon his life, she must be included in the equation
for your future. Some ex-wives are holy terrors, but
it's no good crying "he *should* have told me!"
There are some things a girl has to figure out for
herself—and the sooner the better.

Before a couple starts living together, the machi-
nations of a flaky "ex" can be kind of cute. ("You
poor darling, how you must have suffered with that
witch! And have you noticed how much sweeter I
am than she?") But after the knot is tied or the mortgage papers signed? Let's just say loving the bag-
gage that comes with the man you love can put a
strain on any woman's emotional capacity.

Young women who are dazed and deluded about
this *before* they commit themselves are apt to be
writing an agony aunt soon afterward. "Brace yourself" is what I usually advise. Plan a strategy. (Two
telephones? An answering machine to screen all
calls? A guard dog? Life in another state or country?) But above all—and gritting your teeth if necessary—maintain a dignified and united front with
your husband or lover until the maddened "ex" realizes she really is outnumbered and gives up the
fight.

She writes: *"His five-year-old spends every other*
weekend with us. He gives her anything she wants,
and whatever she wants to do takes precedence over

my wishes. It just isn't fair. How long should I put up with it?''

I reply: *"You will have to put up with it until the child grows up. Or you do.''*

I receive letters like this about a dozen times a month, and I always ask the writer if she would love her husband or lover more if he were the sort of man who could abandon the offspring from his previous relationships.

If the man you love has children from a former union, and you accept him fully, you have no choice but to accept them too. This is easier to do when you realize that no matter how dreadfully behaved those kids are, they're also terribly confused and hurt by the breakup of their home. Woo his children. Win the children and learn to enjoy them. Remember, unlike adults, children change from day to day. How they change can be influenced by you and, with a little luck, improved.

In-Laws

She writes: *"I am married to a man I love with all my heart. The problem is his parents, especially his mother. She is constantly calling us, sometimes three and four times a day. I don't dislike her, but I feel they expect too much of our time . . . and they make us feel guilty because they have done a lot for us. They bore me . . . they are completely annoying. My mother-in-law is always dropping hints about my weight—she has more of a weight problem than I do—and constantly reminding me she wants grandchildren even when she knows we aren't ready for them. Why can't they be more like my parents?''*

As is often the case with complaints of this kind, the writer is lying. What's more, she is lying to that most vulnerable victim of any liar—herself. She *does* dislike her in-laws, especially her mother-in-law. Of course, she thinks she *shouldn't*, but every word of her letter shows she does.

Until she admits this, she will continue futilely complaining and wishing they would change, instead of applying herself to her only real hope—which is to change how she feels about them. Until she admits to herself she dislikes them, there is no way she can learn to like them, or even to tolerate them with good grace.

Guilt stops many women from admitting they dislike their in-laws. (''Nice people *shouldn't* dislike people of their parents' age, *should* they?'') So you can imagine the guilt a son will feel if his girlfriend or wife tries to set him up against his very own mom and dad. When you nag a man to ally himself against his family in your defense, you are asking for trouble that you don't need and could avoid.

A mother-in-law who insults her daughter-in-law's cooking or makes snide comments about her weight or criticizes her reluctance to start a family right away is really no more significant than an old vaudeville joke, *unless* the daughter-in-law is so insecure in herself and such a child before a mother—*any* mother—that she cannot laugh down feeble barbs or diplomatically turn them aside.

In western society, a mother-in-law does *not* become her daughter-in-law's surrogate mother. Nevertheless, the language of most letters complaining about a mother-in-law or a boyfriend's mother make it all too clear that the writer has cast her in the role her own mother once played. As a result, she anticipates a recurrence of all the troubles she had as a child (and to anticipate trouble is uncomfortably close to asking for it). The daughter-in-law ends up behaving like a kid again, putting herself in the worst possible position to cope with her mother-in-law's antics should she turn out to be a bad one.

What is a bad mother-in-law? One who cannot let her son go without a fight. More often than not, she has been disappointed by the other men in her life and clings all the harder to the last man left to her: her son. And in a sense, she really *has* lost him to another woman. She loved him first, after all, and to whatever degree she is a possessive mama, his new wife or girlfriend is automatically "the other woman."

The only power a mother-in-law has in your household is the power she can bully out of you. Once a bad mother-in-law sees how easy it is to get under the skin of her "rival," she will gleefully do it again and again, endlessly in fact, or until you, having finally recognized just how pathetic the old girl is, use your head—and smile. Never let the old bag see she is getting to you.

If the younger woman can smile, if she can talk sensibly and grow up enough to understand how the older woman might be feeling, she can disarm big mama. And who knows? From newly established vantage points, they might even start to like each other. Stranger things have happened.

The smart daughter-in-law who is not acting out her own childhood also grabs control of her meetings with in-laws as soon as the ink is dry on the marriage license. Instead of waiting for them to invite her to their home (or themselves to hers), for example, she invites them to visit at regularly spaced intervals, say, one dinner every two weeks. If she makes it a festive occasion, they will have no reason to complain of neglect (which is not to say they won't complain anyway). Then, when her in-laws try to return her hospitality by inviting her to their home every other time or so, the smart daughter-in-law will make sure she has an *honest* excuse not to go. In addition, if a girl thinks her own parents set an example of what good in-laws can be, she can mix them up together sometimes.

Finally, children have every reason to assume anything generous and good their in-laws or parents do for them, they do out of genuine love. Loans must be repaid in kind, of course. But the only repayment for gifts is warmth in the heart of the giver.

When parents do expect something intangible, like affection or obedience, in exchange for financial help or other favors, then they have not really *given* at all. They have tried to *buy*, and their children are perfectly entitled to refuse the terms.

My Best Advice? Think Ahead

So many troubles in love, as you can see, are home-made and created while we're bedazzled by love or other emotions (fear, insecurity, envy, you name it).

Money causes as much stress in unions as infidelity, for instance, yet even as I write these words there are women out there about to throw their lot in with men whose economic status is vague as well as women who, on the eve of their weddings, have no idea how they and their mates will manage their joint finances.

How unromantic, you say? You bet. I am as unromantic as mortgages, repayments on a car, legal fees, doctors' bills, food, rent, and all the other worldly thorns that will make trouble tomorrow for today's love—unless you have the sense to bring them out in the open and take them into account ahead of time.

Dear "In Pain,"

Lovemaking slows down in relationships. It would have to, wouldn't it? Or nothing else would ever get done. But when it drops to the point where one of the lovers needs more, there is a problem. Assuming your boyfriend is in good health, the cause of his sexual lethargy could, as you have suggested, be the scary responsibility of starting his own business. A tired, distracted man is not likely to be in the mood for great extended lovemaking.

When you say he rises to the occasion only once a week "if you're lucky," I assume you have tried making some luck of your own. Slow, sensual, seductive caresses could help relax him. Try massage, for example, and moves more voluptuous than aggressively sexy. With all he has to worry about at work, relaxation at home would be a whole lot sexier than arousal which, like it or not, he may be getting, short and sharp and simply, from his little collection of porn.

Mind you, it is equally likely he's forgotten all about the girlie magazine and porn video you found. Have you thought they could matter a lot more to you than they do to him? Sometimes porn can be a problem, yes, but I suspect it is not one in your case, and I hope you do not let it distract you from your lover's well-being or your own.

Could you possibly cheerfully share his sexy mag and video? Don't even try if the idea repels you. But one way or another you will eventually have to bring what you found out into the open because it is secretly bothering you. Solitary distress is infinitely more destructive to a loving union than a little solitary masturbation.

Bear in mind that confrontation can be worse than silence. It won't lead to mutual understanding unless you set about it with genuine concern and affection. Whenever two people square off for a fearless heart-to-heart, they must both be prepared to calmly hear things they would rather not know. High-pitched accusations do more harm than good. They lead to overstatement in the heat of anger, and drive men, who do not as a rule take to scenes, into a corner or out

the door. So calm down, find or create an atmosphere of quiet trust, and talk to him about his deeper self, his worries, and incidentally, if you need to, about the porn you found.

**Go in peace,
Irma**

Agony Aunt's Work Sheet

1. If pornography is "bad," (a) is it *always* bad? (b) If a man is turned on by it, is he a "bad" man? (c) If a woman is turned on by it, is she "bad"? (d) If a couple enjoy it in the privacy of their home, are they "bad" people?

2. *Can* there be love without trouble?

3. What problems have you known for yourself or observed in the marriages and love affairs of others, starting with the *least* urgent?

4. Do you believe that for *every* problem in love there is always a fair solution (by that, I mean a solution that does not require either lover to surrender self-esteem, hope, or principles to the other lover)?

5. Is love more important than self-esteem, hope, and principles?

6. Name what is left of love if you take away one partner's self-esteem or hope. Start with the *most* important.

7. How would you answer "In Pain's" letter?

PROBLEM FIVE

• • • • • • • • •

What Are the Odds of Happiness with a Married Man?

Dear Irma,

I'm twenty-five years old. Last year I met the man of my dreams. He's sensitive and caring. He earns good money, and he's a great lover. The only trouble is, he's married. Friends say his wife is spiteful, always trashing her husband and saying hurtful things about him. They have no love life at all anymore. He only stays in the marriage for his two children. They are ten and thirteen. Don't tell me to drop him because I love him. All I want is to be with him for the rest of my life.

"The Other Woman"

"The Other Woman" has presented me with what is to some degree a moral issue. Her letter is concerned not merely with her emotions but also with society's institutions and traditions. Problems of this nature compel even the least judgmental agony aunt to clarify where she stands in general before looking at the specific case in front of her. So here goes.

Monogamy

I've given a lot of thought to monogamy. Having never signed up for it, I have probably thought about it more than those who take it for granted as a way of life. And I have come to the conclusion that romantic monogamy—love exclusively between one man and one woman—is a luxury product of an established, relatively successful race. We can live without it. Only, we'd really rather not.

Other animals couple under the blind imperative to perpetuate their species. They are driven to breed as they are to eat, drink, or breathe—by their survival instinct and *not* by what we call love. In the dark primeval night, when life was hard and our preeminence in the world less certain, humankind must have been driven to mate by the same innate urge. The continuation of our species depended on it.

Thus, caveman fell for cavewomen because females could supply babies, and babies were the future. Cavewomen, in turn, "cleaved unto" the best provider they could attract for as long as he brought home the bacon. That gave their offspring a better chance of surviving (and passing on their willful, overbearing genes to succeeding generations).

Hardly the plot for a romance novel, I know. Yet, we ought to be grateful that our distant forebears managed without the mushy "till death do us part" stuff. If they had spent their time in single courtships followed by exclusive unions, far fewer offspring would have been born to outlive them. And you, I, "The Other Woman," her lover, his wife, and perhaps even humanity as we know it wouldn't be here right now.

Romantic, one-on-one *love*-love is neither a biological imperative nor a God-given right—although, like art and music, it is probably rooted in mysticism. By painting a gazelle on a rock face, primitive humans asked their gods for success in hunting. Their artwork made their prayers more powerful, more meaningful, and magical. And over the ages, humankind's appeals to unknown forces became increasingly complex and beautiful. They became cathedrals and religions, portraits that outlived the sitter, hymns, symphonies, and countless rituals for requesting everything from fertility to forgiveness. So why not create a comparable rite to fulfill their heartfelt yearning for a soulmate and an end to loneliness?

Romantic, monogamous love is what we came up with, and by saying that monogamy was our own invention, I am not holding it in contempt. On the contrary, the likelihood that sexual fidelity as an ideal and marriage as an institution came into being as an answer to our own heart's desire and pleas to a higher authority seems all the more reason to cherish the ideal and treat the institution with respect— even if we choose not to marry ourselves.

Monogamy may not be necessary to our basic survival, but we *want* it. It works *in principle*. And it *can* be beautiful—although it isn't always. In fact, love rarely lives up to our expectations and often causes pain. But surely that's another reason why every couple brave enough to enter into a contract of exclusive loving must do their best to honor it. Then others will say: "True enough, it doesn't often work. But it *is* working for *them*," and perhaps follow their example. Perhaps not.

Adultery

Adultery is not nice and almost never justified. Yes, there are husbands, and wives too, whose spouses have become—through illness or accident—so much less than was bargained for originally that it would be inhumane to demand lifetime fidelity. But they are far, far fewer than novels and old movies seem to suggest. (In all my decades as an observer of humanity and years as an agony aunt, I've only encountered two cases.)

"Understandable" adultery—which the adulterer is supposedly driven to by a horrible home life and an unbearably cold or fiendish mate—occurs a great deal more often. However, the true nature of the adulterer's marriage rarely can be verified. Certainly, "The Other Woman" is in no position to judge his honesty in this area, for she hears only half the story: *his* half.

She writes: *"They have no love life anymore. He told me their marriage was a big mistake. He says he is going to leave his wife. But he can't just now because their first baby is due in five months. . . ."*

I do not need a degree in mathematics to know that a mere four months ago this man and his wife were going at it. But has the girl who loves him adulterously done that arithmetic or even considered the possibility that a man, whose wife is pregnant with their first baby, could be feeling worried, endangered, and temporarily in need of comfort? Of course not.

Love and common sense have precious little in common. And of all lovers except first lovers, those who love extramaritally seem the least analytical and the most deluded. When news is bad, or could be, a devastatingly self-interested censor bleeps out what it does not care to know.

Some time ago, while researching a book on death and dying, I went on hospital rounds with a cancer specialist and listened to her gently but clearly tell a middle-aged man that his condition was very, very serious, possibly fatal, and that the treatment he was about to start was going to make him very ill and tired. "I see," he said and smiled winningly. "But you'll have me fit to go skiing next month, won't you?"

"*Friends say she is spiteful . . .*," writes "The Other Woman." *Whose* friends, I wonder? Hers would be my guess. Love breeds obsession, and because "The Other Woman" is obsessed, she probably provokes her friends into talking about her beloved every chance she gets. They probably say whatever she wants to hear, either because they like her and hope to make her feel good or because they want to talk about something (anything!) other than her married lover and hope to shut her up. In the unlikely event that they *are* frank with her, their information is still likely to be unreliable.

Friends make bad spies. They have an investment in the outcome and lack the detachment necessary for nonjudgmental note taking. Not that it matters. Even though ''The Other Woman'' makes her friends repeat and repeat and repeat themselves on the topic of *him*, she never hears what they tell her. She hears only what she wishes to believe.

The Poor Dear . . . ?

''They have no love life anymore . . . ,'' notes ''The Other Woman.'' She has received this information from her lover, no doubt. And she'd probably be appalled to know that when he told her he has no love life with his wife, he did not necessarily mean that they have no sex.

If her married lover and his wife still share a bed, a room, a house, they are bound to touch and now and again catch a glimpse of what once turned them on. They will be turned on again. And they will do what married people are by law, habit, and convention permitted—and expected—to do. Chances are that they do it quite regularly, too. In fact, quite a few errant husbands actually have *more* sex than usual at home—some to cover their tracks, others because sneaking around leaves them in a state of perpetual arousal.

Granted, these at-home sexual encounters tend to be more comfortably familiar than chart topping on a scale of excitement. But they would hardly be termed "no love life" by "The Other Woman" or the man's wife.

She writes: *"We broke up ten months ago. I know he's seeing someone else. But we still have sex whenever we meet; down deep he must still love me. . . .*

I reply: *"As long as you continue to make love with a man, you may be his 'ex,' but he is not yours."*

Sex and love are comingled so exquisitely in the feminine psyche that no love affair or marriage is truly over for us until the lovemaking has ended completely. There is no point in even trying to get over the man if you continue to sleep with him. Every time he leaves your bed, you start over on the long, hard road to being over him.

Snared by "Irresistible" Sex

She writes: *"I don't want it to happen. I don't approve of love with married men. But the idea of sex with him is irresistible. . . ."*

I reply: *"Believe me, sex is a lot more resistible before the fact than after it."*

Curiosity is an element in every new sexual encounter. The trouble is, it isn't satisfied as easily as most other itches, especially for women. We constantly confuse two little words that don't have as much as one letter in common—"love" and "fuck." Men don't, or at least not as much.

Although a woman may think it possible before the act, she hardly ever has "irresistible sex,"

shakes the man's hand, and says, "See you around."
Sure, she might pull it off after a frivolous or
drunken one-night stand. But I'm referring to sex
with a man she sees often enough to have started
daydreaming about having "irresistible sex" with.

Perhaps, a few cool cookies could still walk away
unscathed (I have in my time), but not after every
encounter. One is bound to get to her in the end. I
know because I've received thousands of letters
from women who have been gotten to.

Many, many unsuccessful marriages have been
based on irresistible sexual attraction. Most infidelities get started because of it. The "successful" ones
involve an adulterous couple who get together occasionally for a great time in bed with no harm done
to anyone. As you might guess, "successful" affairs
are rare. Nine times out of ten where the woman's
concerned, love catches a ride with the "irresistible"
sex. And someone always gets hurt.

And What *About* His Wife?

Sexual attraction, as we agony aunts say ad nauseam,
loses its blaze in the day-to-day exercise of marriage
and settles into something more warm than hot. But
in a thrilling catch-as-catch-can affair, the sex sizzles
longer. Why? Because it isn't attached to any chill-
ing responsibilities. There is no "day-to-day exercise" to cool it down. Some women find sex with a
married man so irresistible precisely because sex is
all that's involved. And that's fine—as long as she
never wants anything more.

Have I just endorsed merry no-strings-attached infidelity? Am I saying that having an affair with a married man is okay as long as you don't fall in love with him or expect him to leave his wife? Not quite.

If the betrayed wife is unhappy or does not understand her husband's new coolness or senses that something is wrong but cannot quite name or prove it, then ''The Other Woman'' is in the unenviable position of contributing to another woman's pain. If you believe it's possible to build any kind of happiness on the suffering of another, then go ahead and try. For my part, I doubt it. Call it fanciful, but sadness seems to cling to any affair that is causing pain to someone else, and that does not bode well for extramarital lovers.

Then again, his wife could be completely unaware of ''The Other Woman's'' existence. But if that's the case, the odds are that he is one of those husbands whose infidelities make him *more* charming and ardent at home. That is *not* something ''The Other Woman'' wants to know. Nor is it something her lover wants to tell her, which means, in a sense, it is *she*, and not the wife, he is shortchanging.

In either instance, the prognosis for ''The Other Woman'' is not so hot—unless, due to a fluke in her personality, she actually prefers her private life to be theatrical and irresponsible.

A woman who fits that description is apt to be a good deal older than ''The Other Women'' who usually consult me, though, and generally has something solid going for her professionally or in some other area of her life. She never cries on friends' shoulders or writes to agony aunts. And I wouldn't be surprised if she is not American or Anglo-Saxon.

Except for cases so rare I cannot recall them and so remote I cannot find them in my files, I have never encouraged "The Other Woman" to work at extracting a man from his marriage or suggested strategies for getting him out of his original oath. Perhaps that's because my heart goes out to the woman at home, the one who actually does have some rights in this business and who frequently wins him back in the end, damaged though he may be.

Stop Shortchanging Yourself

"All I want is to be with him . . ." writes "The Other Woman," and the word "happiness" flits around the edge of that sentence like the will-o'-the-wisp it is. If "all she wants" in order to be happy is "to be with him" (presumably forever), and he does leave his wife to be with her, how happy can she really hope to be? Not very.

Even though everyone knows of a few successful second marriages between men and their former mistresses, a previously adulterous partner tends to be a poor risk for long-term security or fidelity.

The deck is stacked against "The Other Woman." I genuinely believe that her happiness with a married man will be limited to whatever he chooses to give her in the time he has to spare for her *when* he has the time to spare and for as long as he is inclined to spare it. For every mistress who gets her man, agony aunts know dozens more who were left in the lurch as soon as his home life took a turn for the better.

Then there are those who woke up at forty-plus *still* "The Other Woman." And many more than you'd imagine have rejoiced when he finally left his wife but had their hearts broken when he turned around and married a woman other than themselves.

Dear "Other Woman,"

I must not tell you to leave him, you say. Why not? Because you love him. Then, I must assume that as far as you are concerned love comes before everything else in this life, including truth, honor, and happiness. The truth is your chances of happiness are not terrific when you love a man who is being dishonorable by cheating on his spouse.

Some women actually *prefer* to be "the other woman" and not his resident mate. Do you know why? Because they do *not* love the man, that's why. They miss him. They want him. The thought of him prevents (protects?) them from looking anywhere else for love. But they do *not* love him. They love the attention, the drama, the romantic evenings, the sneaky trips, even the suffering and his desperate lies. They love being securely irresponsible. Although they mind being alone on Christmas and their birthdays, they do *not* mind sending him home in dirty socks for his wife to wash.

Of course, if you were made to be a successful mistress, you wouldn't be writing to me, would you? You want this man, dirty socks and all. So I won't suggest that you leave him now, while you are young and still open to offers. What would be the use? You have already told me what not to tell you. And you wouldn't hear me anyhow. You have not written to hear what I hold true. You want me to send you a magic potion that will make him leave his wife. But I'm afraid I don't carry that brand of medicine.

I'll tell you simply to relish every hour he is free to spend with you, in case they are all you will have, which is more than likely. And I'll tell you not to expect or demand more from him than he is already giving you. And I'll tell you to be prepared for a whole lot less than you want from life with a man.

Sorry,
Aunt Irma

Agony Aunt's Work Sheet

1. What is the difference between happiness and the *pursuit* of happiness?

2. Where do rights come from?

3. Can there exist a right without a responsibility? If you think so, name three.

4. Does anyone have the right to cause unhappiness to another or others in her (or his) own rightful *pursuit* of happiness? By what authority is the right to cause pain granted and guaranteed?

5. Is it possible to have an affair with another woman's husband without hoping or dreaming his marriage will break up?

6. An unfaithful husband is in bad faith with a wife, but if he continues to make love to her and treat her well, is he also in bad faith with the other woman?

7. How many sides has every story of adultery? One, two, three, or more?

8. Write a reply to "The Other Woman."

PROBLEM SIX

• • • • • • • • •

Is Infidelity Ever Forgivable?

Dear Irma,

I thought I was a happily married woman. My husband and I lived together for two years before we married and have been married for just over two years. A few months ago, I found a letter in the pocket of a suit I was sending to the cleaners. It was from another woman, and it was clear there was something between them. When I told him, he said he loved me, and it was all over with the other woman. She was never important to him, and it had only happened twice with her. He swears it was all a mistake. He cried, and I forgave him. We agreed not to mention it again. But now every time he touches me, I think about what he did, and I feel so hurt. I only want things to be the way they were.

"Betrayed"

Ideals are the thumb of the human psyche. They separate people from other animals. Rabbits, lions, and whales are nice enough, to be sure, but they are dull in comparison to men and women. Of course, an utter lack of ideals or any need for them keeps rabbits, lions, and whales from being devastated by hypocrisy, demagoguery, tax fiddling, marital infidelity, and other human frailties too numerous to mention.

Ideals lift our noses out of the feeding trough, and whatever trouble they get us into, we'd be lost without them. Friendship is an ideal. Love itself is an ideal. Fidelity in love and marriage is an ideal. Three quarters of the letters about infidelity that come my way are from women writing out of deep despair when someone *else*—a man, generally—has failed to live up to the ideal they were pledged to share. Sometimes, though, their idea of the ideal of fidelity is ludicrously exaggerated.

She writes: *"My boyfriend and I broke up for a while so he could be sure about 'us.' Then he called to say how much he missed me. Weeks prior to this, a family friend had taken me out. When my boyfriend found out, he was surprisingly understanding. He admitted he had taken a girl out while we were apart. He says he is sorry, but I cannot forgive him. I told him I never wanted to see him again. . . ."*

I reply: *"Your letter comes from another century. Loving each other does not condemn us to be one another's slaves. When women struggled for equality (and I hope they still do) it was not so men could join us in the exclusive prison where we used to live most of our lives. For goodness sakes, tell him*

*you're sorry for acting like a warden instead of a
friend. . . .''*

The Shock of Discovery

Women often swear that they'd rather not find out
about his affairs. What they don't know can't hurt
them, they say. Yet, when a man's sexual appetite
starts to flag at home, what's one of the first things
his wife or live-in lover suspects? Another woman.

In fact, his falling libido is more likely to be due
to lower back pain, ill health, or troubles at work.
But try telling that to a suspicious mate, and see how
far you get. Still, women with reason to know assure
me that their unfaithful menfolk actually were *more*
attentive at home, sexier, better dressed and sweeter
smelling while they were having affairs.

''I knew something was up when he suddenly
changed his aftershave,'' one woman told me.
''He'd never bought his own, you see. I always
bought it for him. He wouldn't even know what kind
of store sold it. So I knew another woman must have
chosen it.''

She had a keen nose for trouble, all right. As it
turned out, her husband had a brief affair with an
airline hostess (who could buy aftershave duty free).
And I'm glad to say, that after some soul-searching,
which probably helped their marriage in the long
run, my friend forgave him.

I really believe that most men are good guys and
if they realized how much pain an infidelity was going to cause the women they lived with, and to what

a degree it would damage their primary relationship, they would turn tail and run from passing love. Certainly they would not leave letters in their pockets or lipstick on their collars. They'd make damn sure the transgression never came to light.

Yet, "Betrayed's" husband did leave a letter in his pocket. Others have run up bills for two on joint credit cards, left compromising hotel receipts lying around, or dropped unused condoms from their pockets onto the bedroom floor. Some simply spill the beans. One night as they cut into their steaks and baked potatoes, he says, "Honey, I'm having an affair," and changes her forever.

The reasons a man confesses to infidelity or subconsciously sets himself up to get caught are all rotten. They include:

1. He's contracted an STD and may have passed it on to you.

2. The affair has become so serious that he's thinking about ending your relationship.

3. He needs an excuse to break it off with a mistress who has become too demanding or difficult. (The words "My wife knows. . . ." have marked the beginning of the end for countless "other women.")

4. He's not a big enough boy to carry his guilt and wants you to punish or absolve him, no matter what it costs you. Your tears, yelling, and withholding of sex for a while give him the hard time he thinks he deserves. (And

boyishly the deluded man supposes that after he's weathered this brief storm, the entire matter will blow over.)

She writes: *"Last month my husband owned up to having an affair while I was still breast-feeding our baby who is now two. I was tired all the time in those days and did not feel like having sex. He felt very left out. I've told him I understand and I'm sorry. But I just keep thinking about him with another woman and it breaks my heart. . . ."*

I reply: "He *was* unfaithful, and you *apologize? Oh, puh-leeze. . . .*"

Women have a pronounced tendency to blame themselves for anything that happens to or around them. Little boys catch on to this prevalent and appalling penchant for self-blame at about the same time little girls learn how to manipulate the great male ego. Later on, when they get caught playing around, many men will use what they know to their advantage and desperately accuse their wives or regular girlfriends of all sorts of neglect in order to mask their own self-indulgence.

Betrayed

Loving unions can survive infidelity. Indeed, it sometimes works as a kind of shock therapy and ends up strengthening the original structure. But it is a very ugly way to make a lover snap to attention.

One adulterer's wife writes: *"When I found out he*

was having an affair, I lost all my self-confidence. . . .''

And another: *''I thought we were happily married. Then my husband left me for a younger woman. Now, I'm so unsure of myself, I'm even scared to go out shopping or drive the car. . . .''*

And: *''I'm nineteen and a student. My boyfriend and I were together for two years. Then he told me there was someone else, and he wanted us to break up. I don't want him back. I hate him for hurting me so badly. But I can't concentrate on my work and my grades are suffering. . . .''*

Whenever an infidelity is revealed, the deceived party is bound to be deeply hurt. A deceived woman generally believes that the man in her life has found someone else more alluring, sexier, nicer, or more interesting than she *because she was not alluring, sexy, nice, or interesting enough*, and her self-confidence is shattered. But adultery causes pain far more complex, profound, and destructive than the sting of sexual jealousy—because adultery always involves betrayal. *Always.*

Marriage (or any other committed monogamous arrangement) is one of the few everyday situations in which one person actually has the power to betray another. Indeed, because a vow, promise, or assurance must be given before a betrayal can take place, intimacy is a perfect setup for it. Promises are implicit in pillow talk, after all, and fidelity is practically guaranteed in the exchange of wedding vows or house keys.

Back in the late sixties supposedly smart, sophisticated couples favored what they called ''open marriages'' which allowed both partners to play around with other people while remaining ''faithful in spirit'' to the marriage. ''Codswallop'' was my response then, and time pretty much proved me right.

In many instances, open marriages proceeded swimmingly while one partner played around like a porpoise and the other stayed home. But when the stay-at-home partner found a playmate too, the playful partner went into a screaming fit. Or someone involved would have a baby, confusing matters to no end. And more than once, one partner actually fell wildly in love with an outsider and paired off with him (or her) to form a strictly *faithful* old-fashioned union.

These dubious sexual pioneers discovered what agony aunts and plenty of others knew all along: Like it or not, fidelity is a cornerstone of marriage and commitment. Without it, the sexiest couple are simply roommates. And as long as fidelity matters, infidelity remains a betrayal. Even if a man's infidelity doesn't matter to *him*, it remains a betrayal— because it will most likely matter to her.

He writes: *''How can I evict Mary from my life? She is youth and excitement. Yet, how can I leave my wife, when I know it would destroy her? She knows and likes Mary, we often have dinner together, and she suspects nothing. . . .''*

I reply: *''Every hour your wife is permitted to 'know and like' a girl she does not realize is her husband's mistress is another hour that will cause her humiliation in retrospect. If Mary were older and more compassionate, she could not participate in a subterfuge so terribly cruel. . . .''*

Even in betrayal there are gentlemanly rules of conduct, and a man who observes them has a far better chance of being forgiven, if and when a day of reckoning arrives.

Pain, Pain, and More Pain

Fidelity is absolute. A man (or woman) is or is not faithful, and which it will be is in his (or her) control. But there are degrees of infidelity—the one-night stand, the foreign-travel affair, the off-and-on secretary, the longtime mistress, the illicit establishment sometimes including a child—and each involves a different level of extramarital commitment. (Fantasies and dreams are uncontrollable and don't count. If they did, there could be no fidelity on earth.)

Theoretically, infidelity of a lesser degree ought to be relatively easy to forgive. But because it strikes so deep for psychological reasons, no infidelity is ever as easily forgotten or gotten over as the unfaithful person supposes.

Whenever two people love and make love, secrets are shared between them: little ones and big ones, intimate secrets, secrets beyond words, secret fears, secret wishes, silly secrets. By marrying or making a firm commitment to be together, they go one step farther and entrust their most secret selves to each other. Some of the misery of infidelity comes from the realization that one's secrets as well as the trust and faith it took to share them have been treated with contempt.

Infidelity also contains grubby little seeds of humiliation. The deceived woman suspects (perhaps with reason) that outsiders must have known what was going on, whispered about it, and called her "the poor sucker" for trusting a philandering man. She feels a perfect fool for trusting "that traitor." She had been so sure, so eager, so hopeful. But now the wishful thinking that once dressed him in shining armor has come home to roost as disappointment.

I happen to believe that with the possible exception of criminal fraud, each of us is responsible for our own disappointment. By and large, we find ourselves alone at the party because we counted on someone else to come without waiting for him to RSVP (or even telling him he was invited).

However, it will do no good at all to tell a disappointed woman that she's disappointed because she wanted more from Mister Wonderful than she had reason to expect or more than he was up to (and possibly more than was humanly possible). She will be in no mood to listen to that message until the hurt has subsided.

From what women like "Betrayed" tell me, learning that a philandering husband used the couple's own bed for his extramarital sex makes the fact of infidelity infinitely more painful. But an insensitive brute who lays everything open to the scorn of a rival, right down to the resident woman's taste in drapes and linen, is the exception. By imagining your mate spilling intimate details to an outsider, you'll increase your agony immeasurably—and often unnecessarily. Many adulterous men prefer not to mention their wives or steady girlfriends to the "other woman," and nobly manage to keep their mouths shut even when their mistress is doing her best to make him talk. To add to our pain by thinking he must be blabbing is hardly rational, but love is hardly rational in the first place.

He Cried

She writes: *"I've been going out with my boyfriend for nearly a year. He constantly tells me he couldn't live without me. I just don't feel the same way. I don't feel 'in love' with him. But every time I try to leave, he begs me to stay, and he cries. What can I do?"*

I reply: *"Pass him a box of tissues and get out while you can. . . ."*

She writes: *"He is very dependent and has even threatened suicide if I leave. I am lucky to have a boyfriend who loves me so much, but I feel trapped. I don't know what to do. . . ."*

I reply: *"Let me tell you what not to do: Never, ever submit to blackmail. If someone puts his life in your hands, hand it back to him. That's not love. That's tyranny. Love makes two stronger together than apart. Your boyfriend is dominating you through his weakness."*

"He cried . . ." says "Betrayed," and I can practically hear her awe. The scarcity value of a man's tears makes them seem so much more meaningful than those we women shed more generously. But crying is a highly overrated measure of emotion for either sex and a decidedly unreliable gauge of a man's (or woman's) sincerity. Crocodiles cry too, you know.

And people cry out of frustration, fear, or self-pity as well as remorse. It is bad enough when a woman is blinded by her own tears; but to be blinded by his tears is going too far into maudlin indulgence. I wish I had a dollar for every time a troubled woman has jumped right back into the frying pan because "he cried."

Tears shed too often lose their power to persuade. Consequently, it's a very short hop from crying to suicide threats, which are the most wicked weapon of an unhappy man or woman and as far from a measure of love as a guillotine is from a butter knife. Only the tears of a child are worthy in themselves and demand attention.

Of course, you may see your mate as a child. You may treat him as an undersized weakling who cannot cope without you, and he may keep reinforcing that vision with tears and talk of suicide. If that's the case, then you really are trapped and will stay that way until one of you has the guts to break the spell and free you both.

When Women Cheat

About a quarter of my letters on the topic of infidelity are from women who have been unfaithful themselves.

One writes: *"After nearly ten years of marriage, I've fallen in love with a man I've worked with for some time. . . ."*

And another: *"You may not think being unfaithful is such a dreadful thing in this day and age, but I'm finding it traumatic. I always thought I loved my husband. I have an adorable baby and a strict religious background, and I have fallen in love with a man I met in the church choir. . . ."*

And: *"My boss is everything I ever wanted in a man. I still love my husband, but . . ."*

Apparently pashas knew what they were doing when they locked their harems. Female fidelity appears to depend in large measure upon opportunity. More times than not, the infidelities I hear about are happening with a man at work. But it isn't just the workplace that provides temptation.

One woman writes: *"I am having sex with my boyfriend's brother. I feel bad, but I love him. . . ."*

And another: *"My father-in-law and I have started a sexual relationship. I still love my husband in a way. But his father is a sensational, exciting man. . . ."*

And: *"My sister's husband and I are lovers. I tried to resist but couldn't. She'll kill me if she finds out. I love him. I'm pregnant. . . ."*

Obviously, a woman locked up at home has far fewer chances to meet available men. But given the chance, women in the calm shallows of a long marriage or live-in affair often seem as eager as men to fall off the fidelity wagon. Still, they do it less often and less lightheartedly, if my mailbag is any indication.

While remorse and guilt plague both adulterous men and unfaithful women, what truly tortures the women who write to me is love. Unlike ''Betrayed's'' husband, a betraying wife very rarely says her affair was unimportant. She is genuinely torn between the man at home and the other man.

One writes: *"I am twenty-three, living for five years with a man who is kind and loving. There is another man about whom I care. I love him, too. I don't want to hurt anyone but I feel I must explore more of life. . . ."*

And another: *"Although I was married only ten months ago, there is a lack of sexual interest on my husband's part. He makes me feel so unwanted. Meanwhile, I've met this guy at work. There is something so strong between us. I'm falling in love with him. We haven't had sex yet, but I know we will. . . ."*

And: *"I am thirty, married for eleven years to my first boyfriend, with three lovely children. I get along tolerably well with my husband. We are relatively happy. For the past two years I have known a salesman who comes into the office where I work. He fills the emotional gaps my husband leaves. . . ."*

As I've mentioned, love and sex are perpetually, if uneasily, yoked in the imaginations of most modern women. More so now, I dare say, than in the old days when sex between a man and woman was expected to be marital, and marital sex was a duty. These days, I find myself wondering if women's liberation did not set a generation of females free and then send them straight into the deep purple landscape of romantic pulp fiction.

One woman writes: *"We don't want to hurt his wife and children, but we love each other. . . ."*

And another: *"He is serving a prison sentence for*

a violent crime. My parents hate him. But I love him, and that's all that matters. . . . "

And another: *"My sister will be upset when she finds out her boyfriend and I are meeting secretly. But the love between us is too strong to resist. . . ."*

And: *"My brother and I have been lovers for five years, since I was seventeen and he was eighteen. Nothing could be more perfect than the way we feel about each other. Now, I am pregnant. . . ."*

And finally: *"He's forty-three, I'm seventeen. How can I make him stop worrying about the age difference? Love doesn't tell time. . . . "*

I reply: *"Don't kid yourself. In the end, time tells love and everything else just where to get off."*

As far as a great many women are concerned, love is a great absolving balm that heals and excuses everything, including lechery, treachery, stupidity, and selfishness. Love will kiss anything "all better," they believe. Yet, when a woman's infidelity is causing her pain, it may not be due to love at all, but instead to love's downfall.

She writes: *"I am twenty-nine and I've been married for more than ten years. I have an overwhelming physical attraction to a colleague. I think about him constantly and know I could fall in love with him. I've considered being unfaithful once before. My husband was drinking heavily then too. . . ."*

I reply: *"An adulterous affair would merely be a flight from trouble in your marriage. Wouldn't it be a better idea to sort out the mess at home or put an*

Irma Kurtz's Ultimate Problem Solver   125

end to it before you start messing around outside?"

Quite often, a woman's affair is, more than anything else, a way to escape the failure of love at home. Her adultery is an act of timidity rather than love, undertaken because she is afraid to face marital problems that might have no solution but separation and—Oh, horror!—life on her own.

I am not saying that "true love" can never exist extramaritally. Of course it can. However, until problems within a woman's marriage have been confronted and a solution or compromise found, the quality of her adulterous love is always questionable.

In 99.9 percent of all the letters I receive, the correspondent begins by stating her age, which is why I feel confident in thinking that an awful lot of unfaithful women hooked up with their mates awfully early in life. They vowed eternal fidelity when they were just kids, not to mention madly in love. Their brains had the analytical force of cauliflowers, for crying out loud. But that does not absolve them of their responsibility to honor those vows.

Admittedly, I do not *like* infidelity, which is not to say that I think it's "wrong" or that only "bad" people go in for it. It's tacky to be in bad faith with someone who trusts you, that's all. And to be honest, if extramarital screwing around must be done, the frankly self-indulgent way most men do it seems preferable. Why drag in new love to excuse the betrayal of old love?

Male and female infidelity are in different leagues and will continue to be judged differently because women *will* continue to fall in love with their sex partners, and even in this era of contraceptive sophistication, fall pregnant.

And Baby Makes *Big* Trouble

One of the reasons female adultery has always been seen with greater disapproval than male is that men and their families like to be absolutely sure heirs and successors are in fact their own flesh and blood. In the days before DNA tests, when men only had a woman's word to confirm paternity, the ultimate betrayal was to be deceived into supporting another man's child.

Today the prospect of contracting and spreading disease is what worries us most about illicit sex. But the possibility of becoming pregnant still makes the worry list, as does knowing who the daddy is if you find yourself in the family way.

She writes: *"I'm twenty-six. My husband and I have been trying for a baby for three years. I am pregnant at last, and he is over the moon. The trouble is, I drank too much once after work and had a stupid one-night stand. He went back to his homeland where he has a wife, and I never want to see him again. But I think my baby could be his. I love my husband body and soul. I regret my infidelity, and I know it would kill him to know about it. We both want this baby so much. What can I do?"*

I reply: *"If I were you, I'd shut up, have the baby, and raise it with the love of two good parents—one of whom may or may not be its own by blood. But I am not you. If you undertake this course, do it only, only, only if you know yourself to be capable of keeping the secret under any circumstances for your entire lifetime. The truth could do terrible mischief to your child if it came out in the future.''*

Never has the wrath of readers fallen on my head more furiously than it did after this reply was printed! How dare I? A man had a ''right'' to know whether the child he raised was his own. He had a ''right'' to reject it, in other words.

I've thought a lot about that letter, and each time I think about it I also think about a good friend whose well-adjusted, grown son has no idea the father he loves is not actually his own by blood. The father is equally ignorant of his beloved and only child's true origin: an extramarital fling his wife had with a Russian artist twenty years ago. Would life have turned out better for any of them if my friend had confessed the truth to her husband? I think not. A lie of omission (emission?) between a man and woman still seems less serious than the destruction of their love and the potential loss of a child. And that is why I would not change my controversial reply.

Unfortunately, an agony aunt delivers her advice in public where anyone can read it and possibly misinterpret or misuse it. There's always a risk that the unconventional suggestion I give to one perplexed individual in a specific situation could be taken as gospel by someone else.

For instance, a lifetime secret is quite a melodramatic burden for a woman to carry, but under the circumstances this letter writer described to me it seemed justified. I made it very clear that she must be absolutely certain she wouldn't blurt out the truth at an emotional moment or use it vindictively at some later date. the trouble is that so many women have such a large appetite for melodrama, there's a chance the idea of a "lifetime secret" would appeal to the very ones who couldn't keep a secret if their lives depended on it. I'd hate it if my singular advice about uncertain paternity was seen as a recommendation for every woman with a fertility problem to run right out and have an extramarital affair with a sexy sperm donor.

She writes: *"During a holiday in Kenya I got drunk and slept with one of the safari guides. It meant nothing at the time. Now I'm pregnant. My boyfriend and I have been together for ten years and I know he would be thrilled at the thought of the baby. But we're both white, and the safari guide was black. My boyfriend holds strong religious beliefs about abortion, so I don't think he'd tolerate my having one. I'm worried about the AIDS virus, too. I have used my work address because my boyfriend opens all my letters. . . ."*

I reply: *"If you share your boyfriend's convictions, then abortion is out of the question for you, and you have no choice: You will have to tell him what occurred and discover if his religious views tend towards charity and forgiveness and if they are humane enough to stretch to raising another man's child with love. Once he knows, you two can decide together what to do: raise the child or choose adoption.*

If you do not share his religious conviction, you also have the option of arranging an abortion and an HIV test on your own, then putting the whole thing behind you and going on as you were.

Finally, if you confess all and he blows up uncharitably, you can leave him and then have an abortion, or put the baby up for adoption or raise it without his help. In your place, I'd confront him. It would probably provoke an almighty argument, but then I'd welcome a showdown with any man who dared to open and read my correspondence. . . ."

Forgiveness

A man who has cheated and been caught often imagines that there will be one almighty explosion to clear the air and then everything will go back to normal.

"I'm sorry," he says. "I love you. Now, let's say no more about it. . . ." And perhaps she won't say more about it. Not directly to him anyway. She'll write to *me* or cry into her pillow and try to stop being so afraid that he will do it again.

One woman writes: *"My husband had an affair a year ago and it was eight months before I could let him make love to me again. I still can't bear him touching me. . . ."*

And another: *"My boyfriend said it wasn't serious, just one drunken night. I don't want to lose him, but I feel so cheated and hurt. We've agreed not to talk about it anymore. But I'm afraid he'll do it again if I don't come to terms with it. . . . "*

And another: *"Last year my husband owned up to an affair with his secretary. As far as I knew, we had been happy and were planning to start a family. I feel horribly angry with him, as hard as I try not to show it. . . . "*

And: *"Irma, I thought we had a very special marriage. Recently I discovered my husband had an affair. It only lasted four weeks and he has done his utmost to make it up to me, but I am shattered. I can't discuss it with him, because he has shut it out of his mind. . . . "*

"It was only a passing thing," says the remorseful husband. "It meant nothing. . . . "

"To *you*, maybe" his wife thinks. Not only did it mean a great deal to *her*, but she also knows something the man doesn't: Thanks to the amalgam of sex and love in the minds of all but a few women, even a two-week affair with his secretary—or a fling with a waitress from the diner on the corner—can leave that other woman with hopes and daydreams of keeping what is not rightfully hers. Is it any wonder that trust and any semblance of normalcy doesn't return in short order to a union fractured by infidelity—and sometimes doesn't return at all?

Fidelity is an ideal. And an ideal is not necessarily achievable. We're meant to strive for it and to *keep on* striving for it. That's the point. An ideal is not destroyed when someone fails to live up to it. Ideals are bigger than that, and ideals are hard to live up to—which is why forgiveness is part of achieving them.

Forgiveness (to a reasonable degree) is essential between lovers. It simply has to be, or love itself would be called into question; and without love, we'd all be in a dreadful pickle. But forgiveness is not easy—and it does not come quickly.

The infidelities of men, particularly in middle age, are not necessarily indications of anything very wrong with their primary households. Sometimes their transgressions are due to drink, opportunity on a working trip abroad, or deflated ego that needs a boost. He may be taken unaware by the predatory behavior of a young stranger or wonder if he can still cut the mustard. The list is endless and the reasons almost entirely unrelated to love.

However, infidelity doesn't have to be motivated by a preexisting problem in a man's marriage in order to become a problem in his marriage once the proverbial cat is out of the bag. Unless his wife is as wise as Solomon—and probably as old—she is going to assume it *was* the marriage and something "wrong" with her that set him prowling in new alleys. His infidelity simply will not be seen as a mere parking violation in her eyes. It will require tons of time, affection, talk, and reassurance to rebuild her trust in him and restore her confidence in herself.

Dear Betrayed,

You say you thought you were a happily married woman. You *were* a happily married woman. And you will be again. You say you have forgiven your husband. But you haven't. It is no good pretending to him or yourself the business is over and done with. In your mind, it isn't. Not yet. Some betrayed women feel angry, others feel hurt. Either way, the man has a mile or two to go before he can be forgiven.

You say you have agreed not to mention what happened. Is that a *mutual* agreement? Or did his tears persuade you to let up on him before you really felt quite agreeable to forget and forgive? Tell him as calmly as you can that you need to say more and know more about what happened, why it happened, and how he intends not to ever let it happen again. Explain that it is still disturbing you and as much as you want to let go of it, you need more help from him before you can. Let him know exactly how you feel, so he can comfort you this time and dry *your* tears.

If he does not understand and is not willing to talk out an experience which is *not* over and will not be until you say so, it seems to me you will have to take a very strong stand. Until he helps you get over your hurt the marriage is nonexistent.

If need be, tell him you want marital counseling. Remember, *he* broke faith with you. You have nothing to be ashamed about.

Once it is all out in the open (perhaps more than once), the hurt, explanation, and apology will, in due course, lead to the start of real forgiveness. I'm sure his genuine love for you and his steady fidelity will put the incident much deeper into the forgotten past much sooner than you can imagine now. Things won't be the same—they never are—but they will be as good. And what your marriage has lost in gloss, it may well make up for in truth and understanding.

Yours faithfully,
Aunt Irma

Agony Aunt's Work Sheet

1. In order to make a life together, do two people need to hold the same ideals?

2. Fidelity is an ideal, something to strive for. Forgiveness is also an ideal. How do you strive to forgive?

3. Does it take longer to forgive a hurt or to forget it?

4. How many people does it take to forgive an infidelity and how many to forget it?

5. In your opinion, why is a man's infidelity less serious/more serious/as serious as a woman's?

6. One good reason, please, to confess an infidelity that is over and done? And four good reasons not to?

7. Write your own reply to "Betrayed."

PROBLEM SEVEN

• • • • • • • • •

Is There Life After Loneliness?

Dear Irma,

I am twenty-five. I've been living with my boyfriend for four years, and we are stuck in a rut. I'm bored. We seem to be together out of habit more than anything else. Our sex life is even routine. Either he's too tired, I'm too tired, or we just do it like a duty. I fantasize about life as a single again. But everyone I know is part of a couple. If we split up my evenings would be empty. Whenever I think I'm going to end it, I feel panicky. I feel I'm missing out on a lot, but at the same time I can't face life without him. How would I cope with the inevitable loneliness?

"Scared"

"Don't you find," a psychiatrist friend once asked, "that loneliness is *always* the problem . . . ?" Yes and no. Letters that actually mention the *word* "loneliness," as this one from "Scared" did, are rare (perhaps one out of every thousand). But letters in which loneliness or fear of loneliness cannot be found at the very core of the problem or close to it are rarer still.

I've often heard it said (mostly by men) that if the women who wrote to me were *not* lonely they would be consulting a friend, a sister, a mother, or someone closer to them than a snapshot at the top of a page in a magazine. Generally speaking, that hasn't proven to be true, although occasionally someone very young will write to me because there is nobody else she dares tell that she is pregnant, addicted, homosexual, or suicidal.

Frequently, a mother or teacher who might be in a position to hear a girl's troubles is so full of "shoulds" and prejudice, that they scare her away. "What's the point of asking help from someone whose reply will be as predictable as a party political broadcast?" she thinks. And sometimes, of course, thoughtlessly judgmental or brutal parents *are* the problem.

For the most part, though, it isn't loneliness that drives women to consult someone like me, but rather their sense that a sympathetic stranger might be a better bet for consolation than someone close and deeply concerned. They're quite right on that score.

As often as not, a troubled woman is surrounded by colleagues, friends, and family who listen (and listen and listen) to her emotional turmoil and then repeat what they said last time without much hope of being heard. They give advice that is either mis-interpreted or ignored, until they give up in exasperation and tell her what she *wants* to hear—which does her a fat lot of good in most cases. An *outsider's* advice, on the other hand, works like an anchor on a storm-driven boat, pulling her up short, at least for a moment, and letting her catch her breath.

What *Is* Loneliness, Anyway?

She writes: *"I'm normally a cheerful, outgoing person. But lately I have been obsessed by thoughts of death—my own death and the death of my boyfriend, my mother, everyone. I lie awake at night, thinking about death. . . . "*

And she writes: *"I can't stop thinking about the possibility of a third world war. . . . "*

And: *"There's so much pain and poverty in the world. I want to do more to help. . . . "*

See? Not *all* the letters that come my way are from young women bothered by men (only about 95 percent). Once in a while someone writes about problems other than her own self-centered emotional concerns. And generally her distress, which is understandable and perfectly natural, offers a glimpse of what our common loneliness is all about.

My psychiatrist friend maintains that loneliness starts with the severing of the umbilical cord. I think it's a profound and serious element of modern life.

Most men and women who come right out and tell an agony aunt they are lonely actually mean they want sex. But I do not believe the absence of lovers causes loneliness, any more than the absence of sympathetic family or friends.

She writes: *"I'm desperately lonely. I have so much to give and nobody to share it with me."*

I reply: *"If sharing what we have could really end our loneliness, then how could there be so many lonely mothers, lonely fathers, lonely roommates, and people lonely in a crowd?"*

Market researchers say that poor people are lonelier than the prosperous, the old are lonelier than the young, and housewives are 3 percent lonelier than working spinsters. But loneliness is a feeling, and like all feelings, impossible to actually measure or compare.

Nobody is alone in being lonely. Loneliness is built into the way we live. The key to our loneliness is loss: loss of faith, loss of purpose, loss of giving a damn about each other, and—the very essence of loneliness—loss of self.

Being alone does not mean being lonely. Loneliness is not imposed on us from outside. It is the space within where something once was or where something could be. Nobody can "cure" a space. The best we can do is begin to fill it. How we choose to do that is an expression of ourselves, a reflection of our personalities. Actually doing it takes learning, experience, and especially *time*.

People who rush to fill up with something they hope will end their loneliness are the ones who follow cult leaders into cataclysms. They are the girls who write to me pregnant at sixteen and the women who have thrown away their youth on shabby, hopeless romances. They want "someone to be there for them," and have neither the patience nor the courage to sit all alone for a while and be there for themselves.

"Being There"

One woman writes: *"My father was never there for me. . . ."*

And another: *"My mother wanted a boy and she was never there for me. . . ."*

And another: *"My boyfriend says he loves me, so why isn't he there for me . . . ?"*

And: *"He still goes out every weekend with his friends. He should be there for me, but I don't feel like he is. . . ."*

I want to shout: *"You're right. Nobody is 'there for you.' Nobody* should *be 'there for you,' and nobody* can *be 'there for you.' "*

"Being there for me . . ." is another self-proclaimed "right" requiring no expenditure of energy or self. It is a vain, uncharitable little concept, pumped up with ego, generally said in a whining tone and used to blame or accuse. It is a cliché I would like never to see or hear again, especially when the subject is love.

The people important to you are there for you to love as well as you can. They will love you back if they are able, as much as they are able. They will help you when they can and as much as they can or are willing to. But they will not be there for you at all times under all circumstances and in all the ways you wish them to be.

If ever there was a notion designed to increase

loneliness and alienation in our society it has got to be the very idea that someone, anyone, has a duty to be there for you because you *want* him (or her) to be there for you.

She writes: *"I'm seventeen but very mature for my age. I want to have a baby so there will always be somebody there for me. . . ."*

I reply: *"Is that why your mother had you? And are you there for her? Somehow, I doubt it. Please try to wait until you know you are ready to give a new life the chance to be there for its own sweet self. . . ."*

"Being there for me" belongs in the nursery. I am appalled to hear women use it, which they do, it seems to me, much more often than men. How can a woman ever be free if she insists upon having someone "be there" to hold her hand?

Let's leave it at this: People are there, that's all. When you love someone, be grateful when he *is* there. But realize that he is there for himself, to be himself and voluntarily give of himself as well as he can. Then, go ahead and be there for *yourself.* Be yourself and freely give of yourself—your understanding, your humor, your personality—as well as you can.

A Fate Worse Than Loneliness

The "inevitable loneliness" that "Scared" fears she'll experience when she leaves her very bad relationship will not be the result of being alone. She is already as alone as a woman can be, and so are others like her who stay in dreary or brutal relationships because they fear the alternative which they call "loneliness." But it isn't really loneliness they are afraid of, either. They are familiar with loneliness. (What could be lonelier than "Scared's" present existence, locked up in a small space with a man whose company she no longer wants or enjoys?)

No, "Scared" and other women in similar situations are not afraid of loneliness. They are afraid of independence. They are afraid to explore. They are afraid of the freedom to act on nobody's say-so but their own and risk making a mistake.

"If we split up," says "Scared," *"my evenings would be empty. . . ."* Since she complained of "boredom" with her lover, I presume he bores her. But if she is scared of being bored without him, what is left for me to think except that she bores herself as well? And if she is bored in her own company, it is unlikely she will ever be anything but bored in someone else's company or, for that matter, anything but boring in anyone's company.

Half of being bored in your marriage or love affair comes from being boring yourself. And most of being boring is the result of having developed no resources to fall back upon in solitude or share in company. Those resources take time to cultivate and are cultivated almost exclusively during times when there is nobody around to relieve you of the need to entertain yourself.

What sort of entertainment needs no company? For a start, there's thinking. Thought and boredom are incompatible.

"Oh, I never think," a woman I know said to me,

and she sounded proud of herself, too. "I *feel* my way to all my decisions."

That was undoubtedly one of the silliest things I'd ever heard. She thinks for sure. We all do. We have to. She just doesn't think she thinks, and obviously she doesn't think more than she must. The decisions she proudly claims to have felt her way to include two failed marriages, an on-again, off-again love affair with another woman's husband, and countless attempts to find a congenial way to pay her bills.

Could she have done any worse trying to *feel* a little less and think more? Certainly not.

The best way to solve a problem on your own is to think about it from more than one angle, to pull back from it until you can see it whole. From that vantage point a workable solution is likely to gradually appear.

"Doesn't reading daily letters from troubled people bore you to tears?" I'm often asked. Not at all is my reply. No agony letter has *ever* bored me, because every one requires thought. Analyzing, imagining, remembering, and choosing my words is never boring.

Still, thinking remains a very underrated activity, especially among women. It seems too cold and masculine to them. Too *unfeeling*—not that I'm knocking feelings, mind you. Only, the next time you're alone on Saturday night and feeling bored, before you say you're "lonely," *think* about what you are feeling. Don't rush out of your house as if it were haunted and go anywhere with anyone just to get away. *That* really is boring. What's more, spending time with people simply to avoid being alone will lead to real loneliness in the long run.

I wish I could advise every woman who is unhappy with a lover or husband to get herself out immediately, as she could very well find herself a lot less lonely when she is alone. I can't, however, because many women are responsible for more than their own happiness.

She writes: *"My boyfriend and I have a two-year-old daughter. But my boyfriend treats me like dirt, and I wonder why I stay with him. . . ."*

When a couple has children to consider, splitting up is a complex business. Under some circumstances—if both parents are deeply attached to their children and involved in their upbringing, for instance—there are good reasons for staying together. The mutual love a couple feel for their children can be strong enough to nourish a family and sustain it after the grown-ups no longer feel passion for each other.

By the same token, if a woman's husband insults, beats, and humiliates her or generally "treats her like dirt," the damage that staying together could do to the children must be taken into account. Seeing Mama put up with what is actually an unacceptable degree of debasement can contaminate the way children will live and love as adults. When it could protect youngsters from harm today or break a cycle of abuse before it reaches the next generation, breaking up the household may be a good idea. Of course, there is no black-and-white rule.

Money, Money, Money

There is only one reason worse than the fear of loneliness to stop a woman from leaving a man who bores or disgusts her or "treats her like dirt."

She writes: *"We have no real contact anymore. There's nothing much between us. He doesn't even notice that sex with him turns me off, and we never talk. I want to leave. But we have a lovely house, I have my own car, and I'd never be able to afford this lifestyle on my own. . . ."*

I reply: *"If the sex turns you off, what are you doing it for? Money, I guess. And there's a name for that. . . ."*

Materialism hardens hearts and makes people fake emotions they cannot actually feel. Creature comfort has its place in love, but fear of discomfort is a crummy excuse for staying in a loveless situation. That's easy for me to say, I know. I have a marketable skill, and in a crunch I can wait on tables. Next to writing, waitressing was my favorite of many jobs. I was good at it, and I would do it again, if necessary.

I'm proud of the fact that nobody has supported me financially since childhood. And I admit my pride may prejudice me to some extent. But the idea of loving, or pretending to love, or even just committing an act of love primarily for money really goes against my grain. I've never considered it, not even when I've been broke and desperate to pay the rent.

I realize the flesh-peddling business has been around long enough to have achieved a kind of venerability. I recognize that prostitutes are not bad people. I can even acknowledge that their profession is useful in a way. But I cannot admire screwing for money. I find it squalid and soul destroying, and, besides, the wages do not equal the risks.

On the three or four occasions girls have written to me to justify prostitution as a way of paying off their debts or in one case to pay for a college degree, I've given them a sharp piece of my mind and recommended waitressing as a cleaner, safer, and in the long run much less alienating and lonely-making alternative.

I do not doubt that financial insecurity is one component of the loneliness "Scared" and others like her say they fear. After all, being broke alone *is* a whole lot scarier than being broke in company. Nevertheless, there is more holding these women back than that.

There is also shame. Good old shame. Where would we be without it? Happier, I dare say, and kinder to each other.

Shame, Shame, Shame

One woman writes: *"How can I stop blushing whenever I meet a man?"*

And another: *"I freeze whenever I have to talk to strangers. . . ."*

And: *"I want to go to Weight Watchers but I'm too scared of what people will think. . . ."*

Shame is a lonesome feeling that, paradoxically, depends upon other people. "Aren't you ashamed of yourself?'' a mother asks her little girl, and the child hangs her head. Yes, she's ashamed of what she was doing, but only because her mother caught her doing it and disapproved.

Shame stems from what we think other people are thinking about us and how we imagine we would look to them if they could see what we were up to. All of us experience it. But some women (and men too) worry about appearances to the point of paralysis and suffer such intense shame that they can't bear to be with other people. Nine times out of ten they call their self-imposed exile ''loneliness.''

"Everyone I know is part of a couple . . ." writes ''Scared'' explaining her reluctance to get out of a dead-end affair. ''I'd feel ashamed if I wasn't,'' she implies.

She writes: *"I'm twenty-two. My friends say I'm pretty and I dress well. But I haven't even had a date in more than a year. More and more of my friends are in couples. I'm tired of crying all alone at night. What's wrong with me?"*

I reply: *"You're young, you're pretty, you dress well, and you have friends. Nothing is wrong with you. Bear in mind all that is right with you and let people see it."*

A woman alone starts out thinking that *others* must believe she isn't worth very much (if she was, wouldn't a man have claimed her company by now?). Sadly, it doesn't take long for her to begin thinking about herself as she believes others do. (''I must not be of much value,'' she tells herself, ''because no man is after me.'')

Like an awful lot of shame, the shame of manlessness (or "loneliness," as manless women and womenless men mistakenly call it) carries sexual connotations. What do people on their own do for sex? (Tsk. Tsk.) Presumably, the best they can.

She writes: *"Because I have no sex life, I masturbate three or four times a week. Whenever I do it, I feel so sad and lonely afterwards. . . ."*

I reply: *"If you feel sad and lonely afterward and you felt sad and lonely before, then at least it relieves you of feeling sad and lonely while you're doing it. And what is wrong with that?"*

Masturbation is sometimes called the "lonely vice," though in fact it is more solitary than lonely, and it is hardly a vice at all. What makes it worrisome for many of the younger women who write to me is that it reminds them that no partner has volunteered for or been seduced into a livelier game.

She writes: *"I'm twenty-one and still a virgin. I want to wait for someone special. But I'm the only virgin I know, and my friends make me feel like a freak. . . ."*

I reply: *"You have taste, principles, romance, and self-control. Any bunch of people who make you feel like a 'freak' for these qualities are not friends and not worth worrying about. . . ."*

Funny isn't it that in the old days shame fell on the girl who went out and did "it." Now it falls on the one who stays at home alone and doesn't.

True enough, in a society devoted to coupledom and group activities the way ours is, being on your own can easily *look* like failure. But surely being independent and acting without constantly conforming to the prevailing style is a reason for pride, not shame or loneliness. Indeed, the only person as lonely as a woman in an unhappy love affair or marriage is the one who goes along with what her crowd says because she's afraid to think for herself.

There is only one treatment for shame, and that is to stop feeling it. How do you stop feeling it? You unglue your opinions from those of the people around you. You think for yourself, in other words, and then, you look the rest of the world straight in the eye, knowing you know better than anyone what holds true for you.

When you think for yourself, you can see for yourself that there is absolutely nothing "wrong" with a woman (or man) staying in alone on Saturday night or living alone, traveling alone, or staying a virgin until she freely chooses to let someone deserving share all she has to offer. (Given how quickly women jump to conclusions, let me make it clear I'm not advocating virginity for one and all.)

Is it lonely to think alone? Not in the least. It is losing yourself in the common way of thinking *without* thinking that causes loneliness. It is losing yourself in sex, in drugs, in noise. Loneliness is losing yourself.

Finding Yourself

She writes: *"My relationship with my boyfriend has been going from bad to worse in the four years since we've been living together. When I do something he doesn't like, sometimes he won't speak to me for days. I'm twenty-two and he's four years older.*

There's this guy I've been seeing at work who is kind, good-looking, and everything I've ever wanted. He says he loves me and wants to live with me. Can I trust him?''

I reply: *"Never mind trusting him. You have been living with a dominating lover since you were a girl of eighteen. What makes you think you can trust yourself . . . ?''*

I remember hearing a movie star married for the fourth or fifth time say to an audience of millions: "This is the real thing. I'll never be lonely again. I've found myself at last!'' And I remember thinking, if it really was herself she'd been looking for over the years, then she must have been looking in some odd places. And if it was herself she thought she'd found in the man beside her, then she wasn't seeing very clearly. Besides being male, he was fifteen years younger than she, taller, and considerably prettier.

We all do most of our growing up when we're alone, and any woman who flits from one man to another with no solitary time in between never grows up. Moreover, when a woman leaves one man for another, she takes half her problems along with her. Solitary time between relationships will show her more of who she is and who she can be than looking at her reflection in the lovesick eyes of the next man.

As part of their initiation into adulthood youngsters from certain Native American tribes are sent into the wilderness to live by themselves for a time. Each young person must not only master the tools of survival needed on long hunting trips but also come to terms with his own thoughts, dreams, and personality. Only someone able to survive alone is considered ready to work in harmony with adult society.

The wilderness in our lives is of a different variety. I can't isolate every girl and boy until they grow up the only way possible—alone. But I do wish that I could send a single movie theater ticket to every woman stuck in a miserable marriage and to each girl rushing into one because she's scared of being left alone on the shelf. She would have to go to that movie by herself, of course. By doing so, she would learn (I hope) that she *can* survive doing a little something without company.

I'm not much of a social crusader, probably because problems come my way one at a time. However, there is one bandwagon I ride with pride. It is my very own Going Out Alone Society: GOAS. Why should a solitary person sit at home (unless she wants to)? Why must she feel unloved, unchosen, and full of shame simply because there's no one around to go out with her? In the last century, perhaps a girl by herself in a public place would be looked at with disapproval or suspicion. But these days, a single woman can go out unescorted without anyone noticing, much less objecting.

And why should they? There is no law stating that theaters, concerts, cinemas, parks, holiday outings, restaurants, and such are off-limits to a woman (or a man) on her (or his) own. Here we have a genuine, guaranteed right. We pay our own way and can choose to go wherever we please.

''Oh, I couldn't!'' a young friend of mine cried when I suggested she go to a movie by herself instead of waiting for someone to invite her. "I'd be scared."

"Of what?" I inquired.

"I don't know. . . ."

If she is afraid of being attacked by a savage rapist, then surely she is as safe in a crowd as sitting alone in her room. To little baby girls who assume they need a big strong man to protect them wherever they go, I say, stay home, then, and let life pass you by while you wait for some hunk to come along with a glass slipper.

On the other hand, if my friend and girls like her are afraid of being *seen* alone, let me remind them that shame is an unworthy excuse for staying away from a movie or any other event. A good movie holds as much interest and entertainment for a single person as for a couple. Besides, most strangers are much too interested in themselves to pay attention to the solitary woman in their midst. People who do notice her will see her precisely as she presents herself, and if she's a member of my society, she'll be bright, eager to enjoy her share of pleasures, and not the least bit embarrassed.

Regardless of her reasons, any girl who is scared to be or do or go out on her own and who gets over that fear and becomes more independent has begun to put an end to her loneliness.

Is independence a selfish condition? I don't think so. It's the dependent person who sees others as "being there for her," and does not see them apart from her own needs. She is the self-centered one, the one destined to be disappointed and most likely to complain of loneliness.

Contrary to the lyrics of a popular song, people who *need* people are the unluckiest people in the world. People who need to be needed by people are almost as unlucky. Liking the people whose company you choose to keep is good, however, and worth waiting for.

In Conclusion . . .

The shortage of friends and lovers may be an itch. But failure to be content in your own company causes pain. Solitude and loneliness are only the same for a woman who has developed no skills of independence and who is still waiting for someone else (preferably a man) to give her what she's perfectly capable of finding alone and cultivating to share with others. She is the woman who will rush to commit herself to a man and then call herself ''mature'' for taking such a bold step at such a young age when, in fact, the lonely space within her is as empty as it was the day she was born. All the parties, friends, lovers, and agony aunts on earth cannot make that woman one bit less afraid of loneliness as long as she is unwilling to ever be alone.

Dear ''Scared,''

How can a man with whom you have nothing pleasurable in common stand between you and ''inevitable loneliness''? What do you imagine loneliness to be if not the isolation and emptiness you are feeling now

within your love affair? You're not afraid of loneliness; you are afraid of being alone, which is not the same thing. You are afraid of standing on your own two feet with no man to give you an identity as half a couple. You are, in other words, afraid of growing up.

Grown-ups are never bored. Generally, their trouble is finding time in the day to do all they want to do or are required to do. Who knows? Perhaps if you were more grown-up and self-sufficient your love affair would not have drifted into these shallows. What you must do for yourself now is see to it you never again find yourself in a stagnant backwater because you are afraid of loneliness.

You have three choices: (1) stay as you are; (2) wait around for another man to rescue you from this one (and then another man to rescue you from that one, and so on); or (3) get out and find out who you are when you are by yourself—who you truly are, in other words.

It isn't easy, and it isn't always fun to face the world on your own, but after a while you'll start to enjoy it. And in the end, when you do meet someone you want to live with, you'll be a whole person with lots and lots to share. The word ''boredom'' need never cross your mind again.

You say you are together with your boyfriend out of no more than habit. Sometimes, the best way to break a habit is cold turkey.

As an exercise, I recommend you go away to a city or town where you've never been before; check in all alone to a motel for a few days. Take a Walkman, your favorite music, a notebook and pen, maybe something to read, settle in, and sweat it out.

When two or three days are done in solitude and a few meals taken alone in public, you may find you have begun to discover things about yourself and your capabilities you never knew before.

Bon voyage,
Aunt Irma

Agony Aunt's Work Sheet

1. When you are on your own, name exactly what you are afraid of.

2. List as many chores and activities as you can that you need to be on your own to do.

3. Why do you consider yourself good company?

4. Which would you rather have on Saturday night: a blind date, the wrong date, or no date? Give three reasons why.

5. Name six items you would take to a desert island, least important first.

6. Which do you think is loneliest and why: (a) wearing a sweatsuit and sneakers to a party where everyone else is designer dressed; (b) being the only vegetarian at a roast beef dinner; or (c) sitting by yourself on a front porch at night, listening to your favorite music?

7. Write your own answer to "Scared."

• • • • • • • • •

What Are Friends For?

Dear Irma,

Last week at a club I saw my best friend's boyfriend with another girl. I wasn't going to jump to any conclusions, but then I saw him kiss her. I was furious. My friend is crazy about this boy. They've been together for two years and are talking about marriage. I want to tell her what I saw, but I am afraid she won't believe me. I've never liked her boyfriend and made no secret of my feelings. I don't want to spoil my friendship with her, but if I don't tell her what I saw, how can I look her in the eye again?

"Torn"

It looks so simple at first reading. But if it were that simple, then "Torn" wouldn't be torn, would she? Friendship is complicated. Love affairs are actually simpler. Physical attraction pulls lovers to each other, and sex glues them together until shared joys and troubles, habit, babies, houses, and in-laws cement the deal. Then, if the lovers are lucky and kind to each other and relatively selfless, they may find they are truly each other's friends as well.

What Friends Are For

Women have a special gift for friendship. Heart-to-heart talks come easily to us. Intimacy between friends is not frightening for us. On the contrary, we stick our necks out for it. We can't win them all, but it's worth the risk. When friendships work they are every bit as valuable in a woman's life as love affairs. In fact, women today create whole surrogate families out of friends, and they are quite wonderful, especially for divorcees and widows and outcasts from broken homes.

Unfortunately, like all special gifts, our friendliness has the potential to cause great pain as well as create great joy. The very ease and depth of our intimacies and confidences makes a spoiled friendship peculiarly poisonous.

When the give-and-take between friends is unbalanced or shifts, the relationship changes, sometimes turning nasty and envious. And there is no enemy as jealous and spiteful as a former friend.

Friendship is more than one plus one minus sex. We women *will* try to change our lovers and husbands or wish them closer to a romantic ideal (that is the unfriendliest thing about love affairs). Yet, we accept our friends, warts and all.

Unlike lovers who arrive singly and become obsessions, friends can be taken in small doses. Unless we are spoiled brats or bullies who always want our own way, if we can't accept something a friend is doing, we simply regulate the amount or kind of contact we have with her.

I have, for example, one friend I love dearly and would trust with my life, but to whom I would not dream of entrusting a secret. Trying to keep it would half kill her, and she would probably fail. Why should I expect her to keep my secrets for me if I know she can't? Because that's what friends are *supposed* to do? Ridiculous! I'll keep my own secrets—and my friend, thank you.

Bestowing approval and disapproval is *not* what friends are for. Worry on a friend's behalf, if you must. But we are not each other's keepers. The moment you start to judge a friend, or she judges you, the friendship falters. If you publicly discuss your disapproval of her appearance, her personality, her child-rearing practices, or her taste in men, the friendship—whatever there was of it—is as good as over.

She writes: *"My best friend and I grew up together. We have always been there for each other. Now she has a new boyfriend and it's getting serious between them. She doesn't call me as much as she used to. He is coming between us and I am brokenhearted. . . ."*

I reply: *"Right or wrong, when a young woman meets a man who matters, love comes first and before everything. It is not the man, it's love that has put a space between you—but only for a while. If you are her good friend, then be happy for her, and wait. That's what friends are for."*

The friendships of youth are more volatile than they will be later. Young girls have "best friends" with whom they share an intense bond. Their friendship is exclusive and intimate, but not necessarily permanent. Best friends often drift apart as they move into new areas of education, work, and sexual experience.

Maturing girls tend to put romance first, ahead of friendship and practically everything else (as boys do with sex). That's the way of it.

She writes: *"I have known one of my best friends for fifteen years now. We both came from broken homes and had that in common from the start. I used to be overweight and was ridiculed nearly every day at school, and she defended me. After school, I lost weight and got myself together. Now, I feel confident in myself. We are still close, but I feel very nervous when I phone her for a chat, afraid she might reject me. Please don't suggest we talk about it. I could never do that."*

I reply: *"It sounds to me as if you started out playing sisters, the stronger one defending the other from ridicule, as a good sister does. That is a very needy and intense basis for friendship. Now that you have grown up in different ways, the old roles don't fit. Is there a chance for equal give-and-take friendship between you? If you can't talk about it, I guess not. Talking from the heart is a part of what friends are for. If you can't talk openly, what makes you think you are still friends?"*

When the fabled ugly duckling emerges as a swan

she discovers that, along with her dowdy plumage, she has lost friends she considered close to her heart.

Were they really friends to begin with? In a way, perhaps, but their friendship was based on vanity or pity and could not survive her transformation.

While the requirements of romantic love stay more or less the same throughout a lifetime, those of same-sex friendship change radically as we grow older. We have friends for various seasons of our lives, and friendships that come and go along with the shared interests or experiences on which they were based.

Once in a while, we find a friend for life or leave deep friendships behind only to renew them again years later. When two friends parted by circumstances and then reunited can pick up pretty much where they left off, the resulting relationship is as magical and full of happiness as any between humans.

She writes: *"My husband has just informed me he's handed in his notice and is going into business for himself. We have to sell our house and move into cheaper property. I will have to give up the job I love and go into something that pays better. How on earth am I going to live with all this? Not that my husband isn't a sensitive person. Apart from all else, he's my best friend. . . ."*

I reply: *"You mean your 'best friend' has sold the ground out from under you. That doesn't sound very friendly to me. And it seems a little odd you have chosen to confide in me, a stranger, instead of your 'best friend.' Talk to him immediately. That's what friends are for. . . ."*

Whatever friendship is, marriage does not guarantee it. Indeed, day-to-day intimacy can make unfriendly demands and stretch tolerance beyond the limits friendships require. Bathroom etiquette, for example—caps on tubes and panty hose in tubs—can alarm and depress newlyweds just as much as it does new roommates and prevent them from being friends. Besides, sex requires friction, and love between men and women includes sex.

Can Men and Women Ever Be Friends?

"Do you have a girlfriend?" a busybody asked my son when he was twenty.

"Not at the moment," he told her, "but I have lots of friends who are girls."

It is gratifying to see boys and girls being friends more readily nowadays than was true only a couple of decades ago (before *that* it was practically unknown).

Yet, friendship between the sexes continues to be troublesome and elusive. And in the end, it's mostly sex that gets in the way.

She writes: *"There is this guy at work and we are really good friends, but I want something more. . . ."*

And *she* writes: *"Sometimes I catch him looking at me in a way that makes me wonder if we could be more than friends. . . ."*

And she: *"He's a good friend. We talk about everything. But I want more. Only I'm afraid to lose his friendship. . . ."*

She may call him a "friend," but obviously he

doesn't share her deepest, practically uncensored thoughts the way good friends do. (This is something friends are for.) If he did, she wouldn't even have to flirt. She could tell him straight out she wanted his body (if they were really on a friendly wavelength, he would have guessed it already). Should he reply, "Thanks, but I'd really rather not," there would be no harm done. They'd go out for a beer or coffee, and the friendship would continue.

When a woman actually has a male friend, he is likely to be a brotherly figure with whom she probably never had sex. She probably never wanted it.

When she finds a friendly man unbearably sexy, they are *not* good friends—or any kind of friends really. They are members of the opposite sex with at least one of the two wondering whether or not to try getting it on with the other.

And when a girl wants "more than friendship" with a male friend, she is correct to worry that sex could come between them and leave her with neither friend nor lover.

Someday in a blissful future the sexes will find a way to cheerfully accommodate lust and truly be each other's friends, untroubled by jealousy and possessiveness. That will be the day all the agony aunts retire, of course—marriage counselors and family therapists too. That will be the day everybody is paid according to the job she or he does, the day housework is equally shared, and the day equality is a birthright. That will be the day. And if you're smart, you won't hold your breath.

Sexual attraction is, in many ways, the antithesis

of friendship. Friends are comfortable with each other even at their most vulnerable moments. They are free to seek each other out when they are at their lowest and plainest. (This is something else friends are for.) But two people who fancy each other flirt. Flirtation is a game with but one goal—and it ain't friendship.

Flirtation is tense and coy, showing only the side that stirs and inflames lust. Lust knows what it wants, but not much else. It sees what appeals to it, but not half of what it is bargaining for.

Early flirtation is a gossamer thing, based on glances and flutters, and not much more than a hint of desire. In the past, women were brave about initiating the game. But letters from frightened flirts have been steadily increasing in recent years, leading me to believe that, in the wake of liberation, girls have forgotten the fun of baiting, angling, and hooking, of playfully planting an idea without committing themselves to carrying it out.

Are we using what we have earned of equality to behave more like weak men than strong women? I wonder. Have we become awfully, horribly, maleishly serious about *everything?* Or are we simply terrified of rejection? Men are too, you know, and they're as easily hurt by it. Which may be why men who were originally deemed friends often seem oblivious of our flirtatious behavior. Although they could be gay or otherwise engaged, it's just as likely that they're afraid we'll turn them down if they flirt back or ask us out.

Can Lovers Part as Friends?

One woman writes: *"Our relationship is over. But I want us to be friends...."*

And another: *"We have agreed to start seeing other people but to stay friends...."*

And: *"How do I make him see I want us to stay friends?"*

Women who write to me don't seem to realize that it's quite unusual for lovers to remain real friends after the sexual spell is broken—and quite difficult. Couples who were genuine friends to start with and who treated each other well during their romance have an outside chance of ending things physically with no resentment or lingering passion on either side to muck up the friendship. Such couples are rare indeed.

To be honest, alarm bells ring as soon as I read the phrase: "I want us to be just friends." The "just" part bothers me, for it implies that a friend's love doesn't rank up there with romantic love. If that's the case, is she really willing to settle for what she seems to see as second-rate?

She writes: *"We were together for four years. Last year he told me he didn't love me and there was someone else. I see them together sometimes. He is very cold to me, and it hurts so much. I know it's finished between us. I only want us to be friends...."*

I reply: *"He dumped you. He went off with someone else. He's said he doesn't love you. He's cold when you meet. And you say you 'only want to be friends'? Who are you kidding? The truth is, you want things back the way they can never be again. He has hurt you, and he does not deserve your friendship. Do your best to dislike him intensely until the day comes when thinking of him no longer matters (and that day* will *come). Then, be friends if that is what you still want. But you won't. . . .''*

Friendship between ex-lovers is only possible when neither one was deeply hurt by the breakup. Hurting people is downright unfriendly. And when you have been hurt, you do not forgive—or forget—as quickly as you wish you could or believe you *should*. That's why I become suspicious whenever any woman who has been dumped by a man or is in pain at the end of a love affair says she ''just wants to be friends.'' Common sense and experience tell me she is still hooked and hoping he will love her again.

I am not saying she still loves him, by the way. It is simply that when a love affair ends badly it leaves the rejected lover with a mystery to puzzle over obsessively. ''If only . . .'' the dumped woman thinks over and over again, especially late at night when she'd be better off asleep. ''If only I had done *X*, or said *Y*. . . .''

''I just want us to be friends . . . ,'' really means she wants to go back and unravel the mystery of why love ended badly. She's blaming herself and longs to put things right. This is a version of regret, backward looking and not very realistic since she and he weren't friends in the first place. They were ''just'' lovers.

When Men Come Between Friends

She writes: *"My best friend broke up with her boy-friend three months ago. He has started calling me, and he's asked me out. I have always liked him. But would I lose my friendship if I accept?"*

I reply: *"In your place, I'd level with your friend and tell her I was planning to see her 'ex.' Whether or not you lose your friendship depends upon how their affair ended and how hurt she was. If there is any trouble between you and her, it ought to be no more than a hiccough and pass in due course.*

"As long as their love affair is truly finished, he's a free man and up for grabs. As a point of honor, however, do your best never to discuss her with him or him with her."

In theory at least, mature friends share interests of the mind and heart, safe and apart from the burning heat of passion. And theoretically, grown-up friends keep their hands off each other's lovers. However, not all adults are grown-up.

She writes: *"My best friend's husband has been pursuing me for two years. I find him attractive, but I have no wish to hurt my friend. I value her friend-ship. I never visit their home without first making sure she is there. He comes to my apartment sometimes, but I refuse to let him in. I don't know whether it's just a game on his part. My resolve is crumbling. I fantasize about him. He says he loves me, but don't they all until they get what they want?"*

I reply: *"There is no way a sane man continues his pursuit for two years unless he senses that he*

*has a chance to catch you. He knows you're inter-
ested—otherwise he'd have given up.*

*"So, take him, lose your friend, and make what
you can of your self-respect. Or retreat from him
(your friend too, if necessary) until you can look him
in the eye, say 'get lost,' and save your friendship
as well as a good opinion of yourself. . . ."*

Yes, men sometimes try to disrupt female friendships. In fact, husbands or boyfriends come on
strong to their wives' or girlfriends' best friends so
often that it's practically a cliché in the agony business, and it appears that the man's choice of targets
is not always a mere matter of proximity.

Some men flirt mischievously, perhaps to challenge the importance women place on deep friendships. Others may be jealous of the closeness
between women and feel compelled to spoil it. More
than a few men are superstitious about female power
and come between two women in hopes of stopping
them from joining forces against him. Then again,
she may be massaging his knee under the table.

Maybe a guy *shouldn't* make passes at his girlfriend's best friend. If he had written to me first, I
would have told him he was a disloyal son of a bitch,
not to mention a lazy slob for selecting a little playmate so close to home. And I'd recommend that he
drop the whole idea.

But make no mistake about it, regardless of a
man's reasons for coming on strong—and no matter
how strong he comes on—any woman who responds
to the advances of her friend's lover and lets her
"resolve crumble" is equally disloyal. Nothing, not
the ardor of his pursuit nor a sincere "but I love

him," alters the fact that she is wholly responsible for her part in whatever happens and will have to suffer her share of the result.

The Truth versus True Friendship

Okay, "Torn," at last we're around to what ails you. When you see a friend's boyfriend kissing another girl, do you tell her? Not always. Friendship puts other considerations ahead of truth, assuming, that is, you know the truth. The only time I ever saw a friend's lover embracing another girl, she turned out to be his sister.

Admittedly, when a man kisses a girl in a public place, the girl is not usually a close relative. But at the same time, what you are seeing may be a lot less than or not at all what it appears to be. If you must tell anyone what you have seen, and you are in a position to do so, then he is the one who needs to know, as it is up to him to explain and to clean up his act.

The truth, always assuming it *is* true and what you take it for, counts no more than what you do with it. You alone know if there are extenuating circumstances that make it imperative to tell a friend what you've seen. Make sure your motives are pure—that you are thinking of nothing but your friend's happiness and feel nothing but concern for her. If you detect the slightest trace of envy, satisfaction, relief, or I-told-you-so smugness, it doesn't mean you're a bad friend. It *does* mean you'd be well advised to mind your own business.

Of course, as a good friend, it's your business to keep the lines of communication open between you. If the man she loves is the skunk you take him for (as her friend, you hope he isn't), then she is going to need you later a lot more than she needs you to tell her what she does not want to know and probably will not believe now.

Spies are a dime a dozen, always ready with bad news, and in the end nobody trusts them. True friends are rare and can be trusted to butt in only when they can do the most good.

She writes: *"After a friend told me my boyfriend was cheating, we broke up but decided to be friends. It didn't work out though, as I was upset. Then a few weeks ago, I went to a party and he was there. He asked for forgiveness. He said he missed me and wanted us to be friends. I told him I would think about it. My friends tell me I shouldn't get involved with him again. Other friends tell me he is miserable without me and still loves me. I am very confused. . . ."*

I reply: *"Has it occurred to you that you have too many people you call friends? Try thinking for yourself. . . ."*

Dear "Torn,"

Ultimately whether or not you tell your friend what you saw is an ethical decision you must make for yourself. All I can tell you is this: The chances are she will not believe you or, if she tackles him, he will persuade her you have an axe to grind and are therefore not a trustworthy informant. You never liked him, you say, and made no secret of your feelings. She loves him and makes no secret of her feelings. Women in love will side with their lover against all odds, all evidence, and all criticism.

You say you will not be able to look her in the eyes if you do not tell her what you saw (and believe to be infidelity). In other words, it will make you feel bad if you don't tell her. Yet, it will make her feel bad if you do tell her. In your place I'd choose to feel bad myself rather than hurt my friend. Mind you, if I could, I'd have a word with *him*: "Saw you down at the club the other night. Do I know the girl you were with . . . ?" and leave it at that. Otherwise, if I were you, I'd hold my tongue for the time being.

As a general rule, bringing a friend bad news about her lover will turn her not against him but against you. In the midst of her passion she will see your reservations about her lover as jealousy. And, later, if he is as bad as you think and shows his true colors to her, chances are she will be too bitter and embarrassed, too afraid to hear "I told you so" to seek you out when she really needs your concern.

Your friend,
Aunt Irma

Agony Aunt's Work Sheet

1. How are "best friends" different from friends?

2. Name six ways you know you have made a good friend and list them, least important first.

3. How many of those six tests of friendship could you apply if the candidate were a gorgeous, heterosexual man?

4. Name three things you would do for a friend and nobody else.

5. Would you do them for a man you fancied?

6. Is there anyone who was a friend you no longer speak to and, if so, why do you think she cares?

7. Write down in twenty words or *more* a definition of the truth without once using the phrase "I think" or "I believe."

8. Tell "Torn" what she should do and why.

PROBLEM NINE

• • • • • • • • •

Patterns: You Made 'Em and You Can Break 'Em

Dear Irma,

I am twenty-three years old, and after a less than brilliant time at school, I found a job working in an animal shelter. My mother says the work is beneath me, but I love it, and I'm thinking about becoming a vet. My dad is always putting me down, too. He doesn't like my boyfriend because he wears an earring. My sister is the one who can do no wrong. They're throwing a big party for her engagement and I have to go home for it. But whenever I go home it's always the same. It will end up with everybody dumping on me, then I'll get angry as usual, cry, feel guilty, and be miserable for weeks afterward.

"Stuck"

Although problems in our personal lives seem uniquely our own (often to the point of thinking we're the only ones who have ever experienced them), most of the scenarios we set up for ourselves and repeat at our own expense are actually based on general patterns of behavior, thought, and expectation. We're born into some patterns. Some are imposed on us. And some we weave for ourselves as we go, hardly noticing how similar we are to spiders, until the day we discover we're trapped in our own sticky design.

She writes: *"I am an attractive twenty-three-year-old woman who has never had a decent boyfriend. Every guy I go out with uses me—for sex, money, or convenience. It has been this way for as long as I can remember, and I'm starting to be really depressed about my situation. How can I face each day knowing I may never find anyone except the 'users' I always fall for?"*

I reply: *"They are not using you. You are using them to help you repeat over and over again a pattern only you can trace back, understand, and stop. . . ."*

Benign patterns simplify life and make parts of it more predictable and therefore safer. For example, I know the patterns of the big city neighborhood where I live (Saturday nights are noisy and aggressive, lunchtimes crowded), and I adjust my own patterns of living to accommodate them. Likewise, when you know how various friends tend to react in certain situations, you can adapt your behavior to suit theirs or avoid the situations that past experience tells you will cause trouble.

We *need* a substantial amount of predictable behavior in ourselves and those around us. Trust is built on predictability. Learning each other's patterns of thought and behavior allows us to live together with confidence. Unfortunately, like ''Stuck,'' many of us find ourselves caught in patterns that are endlessly destructive. We seem compelled to act out the same cursed scenario over and over and over again, as if we were hoping to find a happy ending for it at last. But the happy ending eludes us, and we end up hurting ourselves or other people because the problem we keep trying to solve originated in our past and wasn't brought to a satisfying conclusion back then.

For instance, the patterns we repeat in our relationships with men often reflect how we felt about our fathers when we were children. Yes, I realize that sounds pseudopsychotherapeutic (and the smugness of *genuine* therapy can be sickening enough). Still, I'd be a fool to deny what I have observed in my own history and that of practically every woman I have ever known, and that is: When a daughter's patterns of love are wonky, Daddy has a lot to answer for. Am I blaming him? No. Absent or present, strict or indulgent, faithful or philandering, he has problems of his own. He is not his daughter's problem. However, he is often part of the explanation for her problems—and seeing that can help her start to change.

She writes: ''*I can't stay away from other women's husbands. I am twenty-four years old and I've never been 'in love,' but I've had an affair with my best friend's husband, a family member's husband,*

*and plenty of other married men. I cannot stop
having relationships with married men even though
it kills me to see them out with their wives. How can
I break this terrible pattern?''*

I reply: *''Every pattern begins with no more than
a dot—the original point on what will become an
elaborate repetitious design. First, you have to think
back to where the pattern began and recognize* why
*it began. The pattern is your reaction to what started
it. Although you cannot change whatever set the pattern in motion, you* can *change your reaction. Understanding allows you to gain control over what
otherwise controls you. . . .''*

The Something's-Wrong-
Who-Can-I-Blame? Pattern

One of the most prevalent patterns among women,
even in these reputedly enlightened days, is to assume that the men in our lives will—and *should*—
take responsibility for our well-being. We expect
this even though men have enough trouble being responsible for themselves. And then, when the guy
we've put in charge of our happiness disappoints us,
as he's bound to, we'll waste hours, days, even years
blaming him or men in general for failing to accom-
plish what was a wacky idea in the first place. Or
we'll blame ourselves.

One woman writes: *''He's cold, and we hardly
ever make love anymore. I lie awake all night wondering what I did wrong. . . .''*

And another: *''We lived together for a year, and*

then he left me for a girl at work. I can't forget him. I go over and over it in my mind asking myself why I wasn't enough for him. . . ."

And: *"If only I'd taken him back the first time he asked for forgiveness. But I wanted to punish him, I told him to go, and he never came back . . . ."*

Blame is wishful thinking in retrospect. It's "if only" after the fact. "If only I had taken him back," we think, "if only I had been smarter or sexier or at his office party instead of in bed with the flu. . . ." Our search for something to blame for a disappointment or unwelcome change in our lives often becomes obsessional. And it's more dangerous than daydreaming about the way we want things to be in the future. Blame does not ignite ambition. On the contrary, a woman caught in blame mopes around the house, wishing to undo what's already been done or have things back the way she remembers them (which is rarely the way they really were).

If self-blame leads to genuine remorse or reforms bad behavior or gets us to *do* something constructive, then long may we feel it—but only when we deserve to. The trouble is that women have an oddly self-indulgent tendency to blame themselves for *other* people's bad behavior—a pattern I believe springs from the days when we women felt responsible for practically everyone in our immediate family and community—everyone, that is, *except* ourselves.

Blaming *without* energetically correcting anything is the defensive reaction of a weakling who wants things her own way but is afraid to take charge of them. It is how a child operates.

A baby sees herself as the center of the universe (how can she know the space around her is only a nursery?). She thinks that what she sees is all there is and that it's all hers. A baby cannot imagine anyone existing for any purpose except to come running when she cries or calls. Mommy and Daddy are *supposed* to "be there for her," and if they are not, if her needs go unmet for even a few moments, Mommy and Daddy must be to blame. Unfortunately, this point of view, which made some sense when we were small children, stays with some of us long after we have the force and freedom to do things for ourselves.

The baby inside the girl blames her playmates and sisters for having things she does not. And the baby inside the woman blames men for treating her in ways she thinks they should not. Baby blames. Baby throws tantrums, too. But what she does not do (because she thinks she can't) is take charge of her own destiny. And what she does not have (because she thinks someone else *should* take care of her) is a proud sense of responsibility for herself.

When a girl wears a short tight skirt and a skimpy top, she isn't asking for trouble. She's asking for admiration. But she can't trust a bunch of strangers in a bar to know the difference simply because she thinks they *should*. If she does, and then proceeds to drink her inhibitions away, what can I say when she writes to ask *me* if she was raped because she was too drunk to remember whether or not she consented to have sex?

We cannot have it both ways. If we want equality for ourselves and our daughters, then we must break the old pattern of holding "big daddy" responsible for us no matter how we behave and then blaming him for his failure.

Family Patterns

An annual chore to come the way of agony aunts is what I think of as mopping up after the "Christmas crisis"—which isn't restricted to Christmastime, actually. As "Stuck" has attested to in her letter, this crisis can strike whenever families get together. Adults relive their childhood anxieties. Grown-up brothers and sisters slide right back into their old jealousies and pecking order. The little angel or devil is angelic or devilish again. The former mediator or instigator mediates or instigates once more.

This old role-playing isn't limited to family gatherings, I'm sorry to say. Family patterns have a carryover effect, with women and men constantly casting themselves in the roles they played (and may still play) within their families. Take work, for example.

One woman writes: *"Nobody in my office likes me. I think it's because I can often see what needs to be done before the rest do. . . ."*

And another: *"I can't seem to hold a job for more than a little while before everyone starts taking advantage of my good nature and expecting me to do more than my share of work. . . ."*

And another: *"I have to keep changing jobs because the bosses make passes at me. . . ."*

And: *"They all criticize me and talk about me behind my back. . . ."*

Mommy's pet or Daddy's favorite, resentful scapegoat, rescuer, outcast: It is amazing how often childhood difficulties are imposed on the office or shop floor and how many problems in the workplace translate into family patterns.

Once any pattern has started operating in the office, the way to change or end it is to stop playing the role you probably played at home. Then take on one more appropriate to work. Don't be stuck-up sis who competes for parental praise (don't even want to be). Don't be good old sis who does the dishes every night (don't allow yourself to be). And don't flirt with Daddy. Don't *let* the boss make a pass, and if he's fool enough to try, handle it without needing to leave your job. If you're the outsider, treat the insiders with courtesy, but why worry about their opinion of you? You are in control of it. Their perceptions will change according to your behavior.

Breaking Free

She writes: *"I felt left out when all my friends started having boyfriends, so I invented one. That was a year ago, and I have now lied about him so much that they are all keen to meet him, which is, of course, impossible. I've gotten away with my lies by saying he lives in another country. I even write letters to myself, pretending they're from him. I want to stop, but I'm trapped and I hate myself. . . ."*

I reply: *"For the first time in the history of 'The Agony Column' I recommend murder. Polish him off. Say he's sent you a letter announcing that he's met someone else. When you establish a pattern of lying yourself into a position you have not earned or cannot honestly fill, you are paving a road to self-hatred. So, put your lie behind you but remember it. And don't let it happen again, or it could become a habit. . . ."*

Habits are small patterns within bigger ones. The habitual alcoholic, for example, can graph his day by the drinks he takes, then put all those sodden days together to make the bigger pattern of an alcoholic life.

When a habit rules, it becomes an addiction. The pattern of addiction is a dizzying and downward spiral. An addict stops wanting her drink, drug, or consoling chocolate only for the moment she is using it. Immediately after its effects wear off, she wants it again, worse than ever. Whatever need originally drove her to booze, drugs, food, or a habitual behavior such as compulsive shopping has been replaced by the need for the booze, drugs, food, or compulsive habit.

Addictions can be treated. Patterns can be broken. But no matter how strong the treatment, how tender the care, or how understanding the counselors, the *power of your own will* must prevail.

Of all the words agony aunts use, willpower is the least popular. We live in a time when the notion that we can hoist ourselves out of emotional trouble is greeted with scorn. The mere suggestion that we would be better off if we took responsibility for what ails us can stimulate outrage—as I have learned more than once when I've thrown a complaining woman back on her own resources.

Willpower is more soundly out of fashion these days than its close relative, patience. Yet, we want fidelity, don't we? We want success, health, love based on more than sex, and sex based on more than games of chance. Well, how in blazes do we expect to have any of these good things if we do not exercise willpower and self-control, if we do not, in other words, take it upon ourselves to break patterns that distress us.

Whether you are fighting along with other people to break distressing patterns in our society or fighting alone to sweep away patterns in your private life, you must know the pattern and its source. You must stop blaming anyone else for it. And you must stop blaming yourself. Since willpower is two thirds desire, you must also *want* to end your pattern. Then, wanting to change with all your might, dig your heels in and fight for your life.

Getting Help

She writes: "*My world is confused. I am sixteen and my life has been full of one-night stands. I go out with friends and get very drunk. I have found myself in the middle of having sex with a stranger before I realize where I am. Please, please help me.*"

I reply: "*You need a professional guide to help*

you emerge from this terrible labyrinth and put it behind you. Don't be afraid of words like 'psychiatrist' or 'therapist' or 'counselor.' These people exist precisely to help you. All you need to do is take the first step to reach out for their help. . . .''

Self-destructive patterns *can* be pathological. But they are curable, and tracing them back to their source is the beginning of knocking them on the head. It is possible to do that all by ourselves, although some of us can use a little help. When a harmful pattern proves ungovernable and destructive, and its source is hidden or elusive, therapy comes into its own.

I do not believe everyone ought to undergo psychotherapy. People who *need* it generally get it sooner or later.

On the other hand, people who take it on as they would a luxurious beauty treatment would be better off (and much better company) without the extracurricular massaging of their egos. What's more, there are instances when we would be better off accepting and adjusting to our less than ideal personal patterns rather than using up precious time and mental energy in a desperate endeavor to change or break them.

That is certainly my friend Lil's opinion. Widely known as a ''soft touch,'' Lil gives to charities and friends when they're broke. She gives of herself, too, and is always ready to listen, to cherish, and, if necessary to forgive. Whenever I invite her for a meal or a drink she arrives laden with gifts for me and my son.

Someday, when Lil looks back on the patterns of her life she will see that all her friendships and all her love affairs were like bottomless vases into which she poured limitless libations. I mentioned that during one of our typically analytical, no-holds-barred conversations, and added, "You know, Lil, it could be that you give and give and give because as a child your mother, that cold and critical bitch, deprived you of a sense of self-worth. In other words, my dear, you think nobody will love you if you come to them empty-handed. . . ."

"Oh, I've known about all that for ages," Lil replied cheerfully. "But what the hell? Life's short, and nobody's perfect."

Dear Stuck,

The moment you go home they cast you as the child you were and you, obligingly, behave the way you used to. You fight, resent, get angry, sulk, and feel guilty. Well, this time, don't play. You know you love your job. You know you can make a career out of it. You know your boyfriend counts for more than his earring. And what *you* know is what matters. Your family does not know these things and why should they? *You're* leading your life. They're not. And for what it's worth, it sounds as if you are doing a very good job of it, too.

Surprise them. Go in smiling. Hear their

judgments with a shrug. Take the old pattern into your own two hands and break it. Do you know how we break the patterns of childhood? We grow up.

Yours truly,
Aunt Irma

Agony Aunt's Work Sheet

1. What would you say is the difference between something that is your *fault* and something that is your *responsibility*?

2. Name three responsibilities, *least* important first, that all of us have in common.

3. Choose three patterns of your own behavior no matter how benign or insignificant—eating habits, say, or the way you act in a crowd—and trace them back to their source or as close as you can come to it.

4. Choose a habit or characteristic you would like to change and then give not one, not two, but three good reasons you do not do so.

5. Think of three people you know well and draw the pattern of their love lives: peaks, valleys, circles, breakups, and so on.

6. When your family gathers, describe the roles each member plays.

7. Frame a reply to "Stuck."

• • • • • • • • •

Life Stinks. Why Can't I Feel Good About Myself?

Dear Irma,

I'm a big nothing. I'm twenty-one. I live at home. I have a job I hate (I'm not qualified for anything else), and my boyfriend treats me badly. My last boyfriend of two years went off with my best friend. And my parents find fault with everything I do.

When I was younger my little sister was better at everything. My parents have always told me I should be more like her. My father still calls me "the fat slob." (I need to lose around twenty pounds, but I can't.) I can see my whole life going on this way. Sometimes, I get so unhappy I consider suicide to end it all. All I want is to feel good about myself like other girls. Please help.

"A Nobody"

I long to take that fashionable phrase "feeling good about myself" and erase it from language and memory. I'd be a very happy agony aunt if I never had to read it again.

"Feeling good about myself" is another new cliché, and a cliché, new or old, is a dopey way to say something that, when all is said and done, feels sort of, vaguely, like, you know, almost right. Use a cliché and you stop thinking about what's at stake and what you, and only you, want to say for yourself.

I detest the very sound of "feeling good about myself." If you do feel good about yourself and say so, you seem smug and self-centered. If you "feel bad about yourself," you sound whiny and self-pitying. But what I like least of all is the unmitigated selfishness of the phrase.

A beauty queen "feels good about herself" as she is being raised over her competitors. A movie star "feels good about himself" now that he is free of the wife he dumped for the starlet he's dating. No doubt, Hitler felt good about himself. "Feeling good about myself" leaves little room for feeling much of anything for anybody else. And it gives the impression of a finished job—as if "feeling good about oneself" entitles a girl to stop striving for new goals or paying attention to anything that might shake her up in any way.

In truth, acquiring and hanging onto self-esteem—which is as close as anyone needs to come to "feeling good about herself"—is a lifetime pursuit.

Self-esteem is the result of believing *in* yourself, taking on new challenges, and looking forward to tomorrow. It comes when you do good, when you appreciate the good in the world around you, when you feel good in general or feel good about other people and forget about "feeling good about yourself."

You Won't Find Self-Esteem by Altering Your Appearance

"Self-esteem," meaning simply a fair and good opinion of oneself, is not derived from comparisons with others, least of all physical ones. If it were, how could any woman achieve it in a world with Cindy Crawford in it? For that matter, if outward appearances were all that counted, Ms. Crawford herself might have trouble maintaining her self-esteem. After all, the face, features, hair, and body looking down from every second billboard are not *quite* what she sees in the mirror each morning. Her image is enhanced by makeup artists, hairstylists, lighting experts, and photographic methods.

She writes: *"I am thinking about having cosmetic surgery to enlarge my bust, but I'm rather worried about it. . . ."*

I reply: *"All I can say is there are many fulfilled and happy flat-chested women in this world as there are miserable C-cups. . . ."*

A few years back, we women squawked to high heaven about how dehumanizing it was for men to see us merely as sex objects. Well, I suspect we are guilty of the same crime. We see ourselves as objects, too: objects of fashion, objects of envy, and gleaming, impenetrable objects of desire. More and more of the young women who write to me are emulating those objects and expressing their willingness to do *anything*, including going under a surgeon's knife, to "improve" their appearance. Their confidence and opinion of themselves is based almost entirely on how they look. Is it any wonder the men who come on to them are also mainly interested in their looks?

I realize that looks have always turned a man's head, but very few men care *what* a woman wears (unless it is too tight or not tight enough). It is women who set most of the standards for what is fashionable and attractive. Unfortunately, in an age when we have more freedom to find and express our true selves than ever before, we are not striving to uncover our own idiosyncratic charms or maximize each woman's individual virtues. Instead, our standards for feminine beauty have become more exclusive than ever, more strict, unimaginative, authoritarian, and artificial.

The vast majority of women are not designed by nature to appear on the cover of *Cosmopolitan* magazine. And those few who are the fashion flavor of the month or year are not automatically happy as a result. I have read the heartaches of enough pretty women to be convinced that one of the last places to look for self-esteem is in a mirror.

"Dear Irma," they write, "friends tell me I am beautiful. . . ." or "I am a model and guys are always hitting on me. . . ." or "I'm not being vain when I say I'm pretty, so why, why, why am I so unhappy and insecure?" Because it is practically impossible for a beauty to be seen as anything *but* beautiful, and any girl who thinks it must be fun to be seen only for her beauty needs her wee little head examined.

When it comes to the stable love and family life most women say they want, beautiful women have such a bad track record that one might actually consider their extreme good looks a handicap, blighting their chances for long-range contentment. Not only does high-gloss beauty pass awfully fast, but the eyes of a lover soon become accustomed to it. If it was all that drew him to her in the first place, he will immediately start trying to find it again—with someone else.

And that is frequently the case with the high-profile men who attach themselves to famous beauties. They seem to fall into two categories: (1) rich collectors of pretty women, along with other pretty things; or (2) professional glamour guys as dependent on public admiration for self-esteem and as vulnerable to changes in fashion as she is—and equally shaky inside.

The majority of perfectly able-bodied, sexy, humorous, adorable men may do a double take for beauty, but they choose "to have and to hold" someone more approachable and *human*, someone who is less of a trophy and not so all-fire dazzling to every man who passes by.

Still, young women race to mold themselves into shallow, constricting versions of how they *should* look. They refuse to accept, much less embrace, the many divinely different shapes the human form takes. They turn a deaf ear to all assurances that women can be plump and beautiful, flat chested and beautiful, beautiful with cellulite thighs or downy upper lips.

I have before me, for example, the photograph of a girl whose letter assures me "facial hair is ruining my sex life." I have studied this glossy snapshot. I've squinted and peered at it, and I can see nothing except a fresh, young, pretty face. There is perhaps just a trace of a downy upper lip, but I needed a magnifying glass to see it, and in some societies it would be considered a madly sexy attribute.

Another woman writes: *"When I was young, I had emergency surgery on my stomach. I have a seven-inch scar that will stay for the rest of my life. I can never wear a bikini. I feel so sad and bad about myself."*

Scars that are not disfiguring to any noticeable degree, facial hair, dimples, veins, an inch of flesh here or there, concave nipples, convex navels, freckles, thick ankles, thin arms—you name it and someone somewhere has written in to say it is ruining her sex life and preventing her from "feeling good about herself." The funny thing is that seven eighths of those complaints refer to tiny flaws that your average guy probably would not notice from a distance or be put off by once he was close enough to see them. (He might even find them kind of cute!)

Of course, there's always plastic surgery, and I guess I could have recommended it to the girl with the scar on her stomach and plenty of others. But I keep hoping that the thousands who write to complain of minor imperfections are not so shallow and image obsessed as to think their confidence, self-esteem, and joy in life could be ruined by a physical characteristic—or repaired by physically altering that characteristic.

She writes: *"My current boyfriend cheats on me, I know. But as long as I have this scar on my stomach, what other guy will ever go for me . . . ?"*

I reply: *"Call it your 'glad to be alive' scar, and any guy who doesn't want to kiss it for your own sweet sake is closer than he deserves to be. It's not the scar, it is your whole self you need to work on. Start right away, so you can wake up one day and look straight past the reflection in your mirror to the real, solid, loving, good woman within.*

As for the man you love, or the one who will love you in the future: Do you expect him to watch you always and only in a mirror too? Lovers look into each other's eyes. They always will, and that is where they will always see the person they love."

Don't get me wrong. I like clothes, and I wear makeup. I am not a crotchety spoilsport railing against self-beautification. Never before have so many cosmetics and beauty aids been available over the counter, and that's a good thing. That's great. That's terrific. That makes the world a prettier and more amusing place. If a brunette wants to experience life as a blonde or a redhead, why not?

What's more, when a blemish is worrisome and it can be healed or removed, then by all means get rid of it. If someone who has suffered over her nose, earlobes, or whatever for as long as she can remember can afford cosmetic surgery, then let her get on with it. Good luck to her. And why not take advantage of modern techniques to correct a genuine deformity, if she is in a position to do so?

It is folly, however, for a girl to imagine that anything of more importance than her bikini line or profile in photographs will change just because she has plastic surgery. Until she accepts that physical alterations will not automatically improve the quality of her work, love, or family life, all surgical remedies are bound to end in disappointment.

There is always a more central, less seasonal, more logical reason for a girl's gut-wrenching lack of joy in life than her reluctance to be seen in a bikini. Like the anorexic literally dying of starvation and weeping because she ate a banana and gained an ounce, the girl in deep despair over a scar on her belly and blaming it for all that is wrong in her life, *must* be investing superficial, half-imagined blemishes with darker and more profound insecurities. Seeing past the mirror image removes that shadow and clears the way for self-acceptance and the pure, infinitely bright and accessible light of true self-esteem.

A Few Words for Would-Be Models

She writes: *"Dear Irma, all my friends agree I ought to be a model. How do I start. . .?"*

I am asked that question twenty times a month, on average. And my first answer tends to be, "You're asking *me*? How in hell would I know?" I do know enough to recognize that nine out of ten are fooling themselves, though. They enclose photographs, and they are all pretty. But they are not tall enough or conventionally cute enough or young enough or fashionably gaunt enough to make it in the cold crass modeling business.

If it is confidence in themselves they want to find (and to a girl, that is precisely what they hope to find) they will have to look for it somewhere else. "If you must have your inexperienced hearts broken," I want to tell them, "then let love do it for you, not vanity."

I have nothing against models, personally. But models serve only one purpose—to be looked at. They are no more than gorgeous clothes hangers, and their fabulous careers often amount to a series of boring, badly paid jobs in between disappointments. Granted, top-flight girls are paid a fortune, overpaid in fact. But their meteoric rise to superstardom teaches them nothing about personal achievement or self-esteem acquired the only way it can be—steadily and slowly. They often know much less about life or work than a waitress or a mother of toddlers, a teacher, a brain surgeon, a student, or a taxi driver. Moreover, show me a model at thirty-plus and with very few exceptions (two? three?), I'll show you a has-been.

Models are not, in any sense of the word, great role models. But then I find the whole concept of "role models" questionable. It is herself a young woman needs to find, not some imitation or stereotype.

You Won't Get Self-Esteem from a Man

She writes: "*My boyfriend is always putting me down in public, which is ruining my confidence in myself. Also he is very jealous and whenever I try to look nice for a special party, he says I'm dressed like a tramp.''*

The people we love buck us up when we're low and remind us of how perfectly wonderful we are. We do the same for them. But as I've mentioned previously, we cannot hand over full responsibility for our self-esteem to another human being and expect him to cheerfully take it on. That's an unfair burden to ask any lover to bear. Besides, any woman so deficient in self-esteem that she has to expect it to come from her boyfriend will invariably receive only reinforcement for her already low opinion of herself.

Men have troubles of their own in the self-esteem department (perhaps you've noticed?). When a woman does not think much of herself, she increases the odds of attracting a man whose confidence is also pretty low, though he may try to hide it behind bluster and boasting. What goes through his mind? How about: ''What a low-life jerk I must be, to stay with a woman whose opinion of herself is so low that she thinks she can't do better than a low-life jerk like me. . . .'' Or: ''She *must* be flirting with all those other guys; every one of them is a better provider with a bigger cock than mine. . . .'' Or: ''She's the most wonderful woman I've ever met. But if I don't keep putting her down in public, she might start to realize how great she is and leave a miserable worm like me to find someone better. . . .''

If ''A Nobody'' or anyone else wants to put an end to her unwholesome affairs with men who cheat or treat her badly, she had better stoke up her opinion of herself *before* getting involved with another lover. When she can stand tall and feel proud of herself, she will finally attract and be attracted to confident men who feel secure in the company of confident women. Like attracts like (only they don't necessarily *look* alike).

If a woman lacks confidence in herself, even a man who is not very bright or sensitive can see it. She may try to conceal low self-esteem under flamboyant clothing and loads of makeup as so many women do. But he'll still sense it. Her insecurity and neediness are evident in an insatiable hunger for crumbs of praise or a despairing jealousy if he so much as glances at another girl.

It shows in the plans she makes but never carries through, her empty threats and futile attempts to leave him, but mostly in the mean or brutal treatment she takes from him.

She writes: "*I've tried and tried to leave him. But he always comes after me, crying and promising he'll never hit me again. Sometimes he is very good to me. And I love him. We've been together for three years and have a two-year-old daughter. . . .*"

The feast one person's low self-esteem can make of another's is most evident when men beat the women they live with. How can any man who holds a good opinion of himself live with a woman who thinks so little of herself that she'll stay put and let him knock her around? It is not possible. Whether he's a university professor or an unemployed trucker, any big person who beats a smaller person holds a very low opinion of himself, and for good reason. He really is a ham-fisted jerk. But that's *his* problem.

The woman who stays with a ham-fisted jerk holds an equally low or lower opinion of what she is worth. If she didn't, she would get out rather than be beaten. And that is *her* problem.

Because of her complete lack of self-confidence, she finds the prospect of being abused less frightening than the prospect of being on her own. And that is a big problem. No matter what reason she gives or rationale she offers, a woman who stays with a violent man or returns to him to be beaten again is afraid. She's afraid of loneliness, afraid of tenderness, afraid to lose herself in love, afraid to speak, afraid to ask for help, and afraid to know her own worth.

In addition, the rages, humiliations, or beatings reflect the couple's feelings about each other—"love" they call it. I'd call it passionate mutual contempt, and it glues the beater and the beaten together. They have an investment in the violence continuing. If either one suddenly came to their senses and the beatings stopped, there is every chance that they'd find no further need or desire to stay together.

I have always disagreed with the notion that anyone could "love too much." There is no limit to love and no measure. Women who stay when a situation is actually intolerable do not love too much. They do not love *themselves* enough to believe their love is worth much at all—which means they cannot love anyone "too much."

There *could* be a deep abiding affection and sheltering love underneath those ugly beatings. Unfortunately, no couple can see it or use it until the violence stops. Domestic abuse can be treated and cured through forthright discussion, analysis, and a professional's help, but only from a safe distance.

As long as their home breeds violence, a man and woman are better off apart. They will never develop self-confidence or acquire maturity and dignity until the hitting stops. Worse yet, when those who beat and allow themselves to be beaten have children, they pass on a sad and dangerous inheritance—the notion that weakness and brutality walk hand in hand with love.

You Can't Get Self-Esteem From Parents Who Don't Have It

"A Nobody" noted that her parents always told her she should be more like her sister. Countless others write to say that their mothers underrate them, their fathers jeer, their siblings surpass them, Mom and Dad never cared. And every word is probably true.

Perfect parents in a perfect world would guide, instruct, explain, encourage, and never, ever criticize. They would acknowledge each child's virtues instead of her flaws.

They would see her as lovable, and tell her so. They would treat her as an individual and help her uncover her own true gifts, admiring each as a great discovery, not merely showing her off as their own invention.

Perfect parents would cultivate, not suppress. They would bring happy surprises and cause no disappointment. Under no circumstances would they abandon their offspring. (In a perfect world they would not need to.) And for *no reason whatsoever* would they ever break off communication with their children.

In a perfect world, respect would be mutual. Disobedience would be unnecessary because all rules would be reasonable. Perfect parents would apologize when they made a mistake and never, ever say: "I told you so!" Perfect parents would accept any choices their adult children made. And why not? Having raised them perfectly in a perfect world and filled them with self-esteem, they would have less reason for anxiety than less perfect parents.

Of course, this is not a perfect world. Not yet. And there are no perfect parents. Never were. And that is why very, very few of us have all the self-confidence we need. While we were children we looked to our parents for the encouragement and attention that builds self-esteem. Unfortunately, our slightly (or enormously) imperfect parents sometimes missed their cues.

Some even looked to *us* for exactly the same things we were looking for from them. Our parents may have seen us as extensions of themselves existing primarily to carry out *their* ambitions, repair *their* mistakes, or make up for *their* disappointments. Many of them had low self-esteem themselves and passed it on to us.

"My father still calls me 'the fat slob' . . ." says "A Nobody." I want to wash the old boor's mouth

out with carbolic soap. How dare he insult his own flesh and blood as he would not dare insult a stranger (without risking a bloody nose)? He must have a very bad opinion of himself. Bullies are always cowards without any real sense of self-worth. ''A Nobody'' cannot change him or go back into the past and change it. But she could immediately begin to break the chain of low self-esteem started generations ago.

You Can't Find Self-Esteem While Acting Irresponsibly

A woman once wrote to relate how her husband had expressed an interest in sleeping with her and her sister. She wanted no part of that, the woman insisted, but nonetheless invited her sister home for a boozy evening and then shared the marital bed with her. Having left her husband passed out on the sofa, she was ''horrified'' to wake up and find him next to her, having the time of his life.

I still ask myself why she did not put her sister on the sofa instead of into her husband's half of the bed. To set up the ideal scenario for a fantasy he'd already mentioned several times, and then be furious when he took advantage of what might easily have been mistaken for an invitation was pretty feeble in my book, and so I told her. Immediately, there fell upon my head a deluge of letters from furious women. Did I mean to say that the wronged wife, or any woman, had the slightest responsibility for a man's beastly behavior?

Yes, as a matter of fact, that was precisely what I meant to say. To the degree that we are responsible for our own behavior in sexual situations and can predict what the outcome is likely to be, we *can* be held accountable. There is no reason for any woman to expect any man to be more controlled or strong-willed than she. She was drunk? So was he. She lost control? So did he. He acted like a selfish ninny? She was one, too. If she was not behaving responsibly, she certainly had no right to expect him to.

Of course, I always assume the women who write to me *want* to be adult and responsible for themselves. Perhaps that is a failure of imagination on my part. I cannot conceive of anyone choosing dependency over freedom—and holding someone other than ourselves accountable for the outcome of anything that could harm or humiliate us sends us straight back to the bad old days of dependent damsels in distress. I certainly hope young women eager to be in that sort of position know better than to write to me.

You Can't Find Self-Esteem at Someone Else's Expense

She writes: "*I think you were wrong to encourage the girl who wrote about her lack of self-worth. Why doesn't she just look around at others who are worse off than she is and stop being so selfish. . . .*"

I would not dream of telling "A Nobody" to look at those worse off than herself. For one thing, it wouldn't work. It never does. For another, if comparing herself to others in trouble made her "feel good about herself" what would that say about her? To be satisfied with herself because someone else is in agony is not a secure foundation on which to build long-term self-confidence and self-esteem.

Neither is trying to be more like her sister, as her parents keep telling her to do. Parents frequently say this kind of thing to their children. It's meant to motivate them, I suppose. But obviously, the comparisons had the opposite effect on "A Nobody." Instead of instilling self-respect and the will to move forward, they've filled her with self-hatred and envy.

Eye-smarting, frown-inducing, bile-churning, bad-tempered, mean-spirited envy is the most spiteful, tricky, and incapacitating of all our nonessential emotions. Envy, the great destroyer of friendships and families, sucks. And there is a hell of a lot of it around.

Envy is an energy-draining, ambition-sapping emotion that accomplishes nothing worthwhile. "Why bother looking for Mister Wonderful?" whines envy. "The best guys go for her, not me. Why try to do anything meaningful? My parents will always prefer my sister anyhow. Why diet? She has the bones. Why try? She wins the prizes."

Envy makes us lazy—and hostile. Sooner or later an envious person begins to imagine that the one she envies has stolen something that would otherwise be her own. She sinks back into malevolence and a sulky lethargy: "Why should I get off my ass?" says envy. "She's grabbed everything I ever wanted, the bitch!"

She writes: *"At the age of twenty, my life is a*

*mess. I am plagued with feelings of envy over a col-
lege friend who is popular and attractive. Her latest
man is my ex-fiancé. I don't want to lose her friendship, but I feel more and more insignificant whenever I am with her. How will I come to terms with
this?''*

I reply: *''Is she a good friend? This woman who
is dating your former fiancé? See a lot of her, do
you? She confides her problems in you, does she?
And asks your advice? Frankly, she doesn't sound
like much of a friend to me. Don't worry about coming to terms with your envy of her. Why should you?
The attempt just provides you with a great excuse
for feeling inferior. Get away from her and other
gloomy reminders. Put yourself in new places where
life comes to terms with you. . . .''*

Envying big boobs, long lashes, good luck, or
anything that could more constructively be admired
is a waste of time and energy. The envious person
can bring willpower, control, and judgment to bear
on envy, just as she would on any other destructive
habit.

As her own confidence grows, she will be able to
see the person she envies more clearly, and she may
well discover she actually likes that person. ''A Nobody,'' for example, could find that her sister is her
ally in the family and is waiting to be friends.

Of course, after honest and unprejudiced consid-
eration you may realize you genuinely dislike the
person you envied. Go ahead and dislike her, then.
However, if you dislike her for good reasons, you
must be envying her for *bad* reasons. So cut it out.

"Easier said than done," you say? Yes. What isn't? But don't let that stop you.

Self-Esteem Comes from the Inside Out

"Enough already on where my self-esteem is not,*"* I can hear "A Nobody" (and you) cry. *"Where* is *it?"*

"In you," is the only answer. *"Rummage around, and you will find it."*

"If we could but see ourselves as others see us . . ." has always struck me as a witless thing to say. In fact, others see us pretty much as we see ourselves. Think yourself sexy and others see you as sexy. Think yourself competent and they see a woman who is competent. Think shy and shy is what they'll take you for. The most attractive, appealing image any woman can project is the one inside her—the one she's discovered, nurtured, and fine-tuned after her doubts, fears, and resentments have been acknowledged, analyzed, and overcome.

"A Nobody" cannot look outside herself and expect others to deliver self-worth to her. Pride is stored within. What she chooses to *do* with herself and *make* of her life will lead her to it. She must summon up the energy to begin exploring her possibilities. Then she must work hard and be patient.

You remember patience, don't you, "A Nobody"? That dreary old virtue that we hoped to put away with thrift and chastity.

What's the Rush?

She writes: *"I am in love with a forty-year-old man who works with my father. He is married, but he says he will leave his wife as soon as their kids have grown up. Do you think there's hope for us? I know I'm only sixteen but everyone says I am really mature for my age. . . ."*

I reply: *"He's a cradle robber, a cad, and a villain. If you were the least bit grown-up you would see that for yourself. Do you know what it means to be mature for your age at sixteen? It means to be seventeen. . . ."*

She writes: *"I never want to have children. I'm twenty, old enough to know I'm going to devote myself to my career. I've been trying to find a doctor to sterilize me, but so far I've had no luck. Do you know where I can find one?"*

I reply: *"If I did, I wouldn't tell you. . . ."*

She writes: *"I am sixteen and want to have a baby. My boyfriend is seventeen and does not really want a child, but we have been trying for one as he loves me and wants me to be happy. I have never had such strong feelings about anything except having a baby. Please tell me I'm doing the right thing. . . ."*

I reply: *"How can I? The reasons for wanting a baby are part of your inheritance and will be with you for many years to come. The reasons for having a baby, however, are to give it security, a stable home, a promising future, and eventually to give it freedom. You are not able to do any of those things. . . ."*

She writes: *"I am eighteen and have a daughter of eight months. I live at the top of my grandparents' house. My fiancé works some distance away, so I only see him once or twice a month. My problem is I get so bored. I miss the life of a teenager. Is there a way I can live my life as an eighteen-year-old, having fun, learning, even with a baby. . . .?"*

I reply: *"You are no longer an eighteen-year-old girl, you are an eighteen-year-old mother. You can no longer be the center of your own life because your baby has taken that place: It is hers by rights. . . ."*

If there is a single dangerous weakness evident in most of the young women who write to me, it is their tearing hurry to lock doors, their fearful lack of patience, and their wonky sense of how time works. In due course, time takes us all. Why hurry it along?

Young people who write to me have very odd ideas about time. Sometimes they are surprised that two or three wretched little months have not been enough to recover happiness at the jagged end of a two- or three-year affair. How can I explain to them that instant gratification is the body's domain? Emotional pain takes it own sweet time to heal. As for women of twenty-four, twenty-five, thirty, and thirty-one who are feeling desperate to start a family, it's true enough that they can't wait forever. But youth lasts longer nowadays, and families are smaller, so there is time to start one. Their panic is premature.

Practically all the old clichés about time are misleading. We are *not* as old as we feel, for example.

It really can be too early for some things, and sometimes it really is too late. I, for one, feel half my real age but know it's too late to have the daughter I'd like to have raised in addition to my son. Likewise, I'm just in time for a facelift but past my chance to be a ballerina.

"A Nobody" at only twenty-one is still in slow time, young time, changing time, learning time, healing time. Nothing is finished for her yet. If she will be patient and try, she has plenty of time to change her mind, to change her direction, to change the way she struts her stuff, and to shake off defeat and depression before they become habitual. She has plenty of time to change.

Getting Past Self-Pity (the Antithesis of Self-Esteem)

Alas, of all the troubled people who come my way, none is more difficult to shake up than a wallower in self-pity and self-loathing. If "A Nobody" is one, she will bat back every helpful suggestion thrown her way with a cry of "I can't . . ." and then retreat to her couch in triumphant lethargy. Some wallowers need medical help for depression—although it seems to me that alleviating the symptoms of depression with medication leaves the actual causes untreated and unsolved, a brooding darkness marking time between the happy pills.

It is generally held that bad feelings ought not to be tolerated by a good society. Books and whole careers (that of an agony aunt, for example) are dedicated to making sad people feel better. But where did we get the idea we were *supposed* to be happy? Are bad feelings always bad?

Take grief, for instance. It's a bad feeling that's also natural and necessary. And can't the bad feeling of anger be useful, creative, and crusading?

Feeling bad is feeling, too, and the only sure way to stop having bad feelings would be to stop feeling at all. We might also stop thinking to shut out bad thoughts, while we're at it, or avoid bad experiences by doing absolutely nothing.

It's when we're feeling bad that we have to pursue happiness actively, and in our *pursuit* of happiness we do our greatest work. (Naturally, we'll need to discover and change what's causing our unhappiness too.) Every adventurous, hopeful human being needs to feel bad occasionally and get to the bottom of it because each time she does she'll come away with a little more self-knowledge, compassion, and good humor than the time before.

Unhappiness advances and teaches us as much as happiness. Maybe more. Even ''A Nobody's'' feelings of neglect and inadequacy have a kind of energy that she can turn around on itself and use constructively—if that's what she *chooses* to do.

''My mother was a great beauty'' an eminent woman psychologist once told me, ''and I was so plain, she despised me. Then, when I was in my early twenties instead of going on moping and feeling sorry for myself and waiting for someone to rescue me, I made up my mind: I had one life. My success was up to me, and I decided to go for it. That was when I began to make my way. . . .''

Humor Helps

Except *in extremis* or in church, solemnity is quite often a pompous fraud. On occasion, the best thing to do for a troubled friend is to take her away from her troubles for a little while, to a movie, perhaps, or a concert. Make her smile. Pour her a stiff drink.

Maybe if "A Nobody" were here with me right now, I'd invite her out to try on hats. A couple of women trying on hats together is always good for a laugh. Laughter cleans the palate for hope. It is one of the best temporary cures for misery I know (second only to homemade chicken soup).

Of course, "A Nobody" will need more than a few laughs in order to find the energy to pursue happiness over the long haul. Youth is on her side. But I fear nobody has taken much interest in her in the past.

She can benefit from a dose of the agony aunt's consummate treatment, the very penicillin in my bag of tricks: the custom-tailored pep talk. Repetition of the pep talk is required, so I hope "A Nobody" has friends who will pick up my theme and hammer it home. Anyone who hopes to help a troubled friend solve her problems had better work hard on developing her pep talk. At best, it grabs the attention. At least, it does no harm. And an awful lot of doing good is refusing to do harm.

Dear "A Nobody,"

Try this right now: Take pen and paper in hand, sit down, and draw up a list of every

little thing you have ever liked doing, wanted to do, or *can* do. Can you—let's say—sew? Can you cook? Can you sing? Do you like long walks? Do friends in trouble come to you? Are you a good listener? Do you like children, animals, old people? Can you write poems? Can you drive, ski, dance, swim? Would you like to learn? Why not?

Don't you dare say "can't!" If the word "can't" so much as crosses your mind, give it the boot. We find ourselves and all our confidence in the things we *can* do and want to do. So, to blazes with "can'ts" and "don't want to's." That's somebody else's list.

What about getting up half an hour earlier each morning and exercising, reading a newspaper, or writing in a journal? That half hour can be the first in a new kind of day. You have to start somewhere. A new morning begins a new day, which begins a new week; and a new week begins a new month, and so on. Starting with one small step, you're on your way to a new kind of future.

It doesn't matter how you begin taking control of your own life. Merely accomplishing a job you've been putting off for ages will work. Do you want to get around to cleaning out your bedroom closet, for example? Why not now? I mean *now*. Don't say "can't." A piece here, a piece there builds your confidence and makes a whole picture.

To build self-esteem, you'll need to set goals and achieve them. Small ones at first, because first steps are always very, very scary. But it gets easier. You'll know you're winning when it starts to be fun.

At twenty-one you are old enough to think about directing those first steps to lead you away from home. Flight is not always cowardly. Sometimes it saves lives. Why be afraid to retreat from an arena where you are pretty sure you've lost before you've begun?

But don't even think about escaping with your dimwit boyfriend or anyone else who treats you badly. That would be a step in the wrong direction. Scout around at work and among your friends for possible roommates. Start organizing yourself for when you feel you are ready to set out on your own at last.

If I hear you say "can't," so help me, I'll throttle you.

It's awful not to like your job. But why not make the job work for you? As long as you are earning from it, let it subsidize your training for something better in the future. Check your list. Choose something and go for it. Just because you finished formal schooling doesn't mean the learning has to stop.

One step, the next step, and when you take a tumble, up you get. Simply start again. Others see who you think yourself to be, so do everything you can to think yourself interesting and busy and terrific. Soon, you will *know* yourself to be all of these good things.

Unless you need to lose twenty pounds for health reasons, the only valid argument for dieting is to increase your sense of control and confidence. You've tried and failed? Well, try again. Don't even whisper "can't." Don't even think it. Visit your doctor first— to make sure your general health is good— and ask for advice on a sensible diet.

Self-confidence has good days and bad days. Let it. Feeling bad is feeling, too, and a part of knowing yourself (and I defy anyone to feel on top of the world when in the middle of PMS, the flu, or a migraine).

Grab your life. Hug it, love it, squeeze every last drop of experience and joy out of it.

If you know down deep inside that you need professional help to get yourself started, then ask for it: You're entitled to do that. Tell your doctor not to foist you off with pills. If he or she does not know an appropriate therapist, try another doctor. Don't say "can't": It's exactly the same as saying "won't." You're not a nobody, you're somebody important. If you *won't* make yourself a confident life, then who will do it for you? Who can?

Sincerely,
Aunt Irma

Agony Aunt's Work Sheet

1. If you could look like anyone in the world, who would it be?

2. If you were as drop-dead gorgeous as she is, would you then stop smoking, biting your nails, eating between meals, putting off until tomorrow, or any other thing you've been wanting to stop?

3. Is it because you don't look like her that you don't stop doing things that make you feel bad?

4. List twelve of your favorite things, things that make you feel good—the month of May, say, or a bubble bath.

5. When or if you have a daughter, what will you not do that your parents did in raising you?

6. If I were a fairy godmother instead of just an agony aunt and I could grant you three achievements in your life, what would they be?

7. Write a pep talk.

Look for These Other Books From

COSMOPOLITAN®

THE NICE GIRL'S GUIDE TO SENSATIONAL SEX
by Nancy Kalish

Overcome your inhibitions and enjoy the fantastically fulfilling lovemaking you've always dreamed about.

77229-9/$4.99 US/$5.99 Can

And at special introductory prices

THE BEDSIDE ASTROLOGER COMPANION
by Francesca Stuart

This companion to *Cosmopolitan*'s BEDSIDE ASTROLOGER contains everything a Cosmo girl needs to know about herself.

78070-4/$2.99 US/$3.99 Can

IRMA KURTZ'S ULTIMATE PROBLEM SOLVER
by Irma Kurtz

Cosmopolitan's celebrated problem-solver helps readers untangle some of life's most complicated predicaments.

77977-3/$2.99 US/$3.99 Can